Rhubarb Rhubarb

Mary Jane Paterson trained at Leiths School of Food and Wine and once even worked at the English Gardening School – as a cook. Her love of food is legendary, her fare is fabulous and everyone looks forward to going to her dinners. She has recently undertaken drama training and fits in voice-overs when she isn't wondering what's in her fridge.

Jo Thompson is one of the UK's leading garden designers, renowned for her exquisite planting and innate sense of place. Jo has won numerous awards, including gold medals at the RHS Chelsea Flower Show. She is an RHS Judge and Garden Advisor, and contributes to magazines and newspapers including the *Sunday Times*. Her own garden is, of course, a Work in Progress.

Rhubarb Rhubarb

A correspondence between
a hopeless gardener
and a hopeful cook

Mary Jane Paterson
and Jo Thompson

unbound

This edition first published in 2020

Unbound
6th Floor Mutual House, 70 Conduit Street, London W1S 2GF

www.unbound.com

Text © Mary Jane Paterson and Jo Thompson, 2020
Illustrations © Laura Jazwinski
Diagrams © Jo Thompson
Photographs © Mary Jane Paterson and Jo Thompson

Text Design by carrdesignstudio.com

A CIP record for this book is available from the British Library

ISBN 978-1-78352-870-7 (hardback)
ISBN 978-1-78352-871-4 (ebook)

Printed in Slovenia by DZS Grafik

1 3 5 7 9 8 6 4 2

Thank you to our families and thank you to our dogs for taking us on the walks where it all began …

Contents

Tulips and lemon cake

Dear Gardener,

As you know I LOVE tulips. Tulips are my favourite flower. The planting of them, however, terrifies me. You see, as a virgin gardener, the thought of digging holes in my flower bed is simply scary. I know I sound idiotic but I just need some planting advice and to know if you think they are better in pots or scattered over the garden. I feel they are more formal than that. I just don't understand how you avoid all the other bulbs and roots. Thanks to you I've got hundreds of bulbs to plant, and I am grateful for them, especially at the promise of a wonderful spring morning with ramrod-straight tulips staring up at a blue sky from their pots. I want to plant them myself but am scared of going wrong… Advice? And should we peruse the history of the noble tulip? Do you know the Dutch story in detail – you know, how tulips were once worth a fortune, etc etc…

Cook

Dear Cook,

Borders and beds, pots and planters – wherever there's a nook. I pack 'em much in.

The most important thing is not to allow tulip bulbs to get soggy. It's common sense if you think about it: look at the bulb and imagine it sitting in our Wealden clay for five months, waiting to bloom. Disaster. So, if it's been raining for days on end, as it has been for what seems like weeks here, just be patient and wait a while. Tulip bulbs won't come to any harm by going in a few weeks late, as long as they have been stored somewhere cool and dry. I confess to planting in January a couple of years ago, just because up until then I couldn't find a nice enough day to go outside. Bulb planters really take the hard work out of the job – and bulb planters with long handles (I reckon devised for the infirm) are actually a stroke of genius: no bending down, no muddy knees and the bulbs get planted to the right depth. As for the other plants, I've been telling you for ever: just plant the bulbs where there aren't plants – it is that simple, I promise you. I know you're worried about existing bulbs, but if you take a photo of them when they're flowering, you'll have a pretty good idea. I know it's a bit of a faff but it will save you the irritation of slicing a happy bulb in two.

Anna Pavord wrote the seminal work on the tulip – a book called, you guessed it, *The Tulip*. She describes how, when it arrived from Turkey, the tulip took Western Europe by storm and almost drove people crazy in their anguish and desperation to collect prize specimens. You can imagine it: such an exotic, sturdy yet delicate flower, with stems taking their own shape in vases. My

favourite combination of the moment is 'Jimmy', 'Cairo' and 'Ronaldo': toffee-coloured Cairo seems weird, but when you put it with purple and burgundy and deep red – sumptuous.

The best of the best of the best has to be 'La Belle Epoque' – think damask fabrics and Colefax and Fowler circa 1983. I promise I'll remind you in a few months, when it's bulb-ordering time.

Are you out in the garden? I tried calling yesterday but I guessed you must be still outside in this fab sunshine celebrating the emergence of your tulip bulbs – the idea you mentioned on the phone of holding a tulip festival certainly is an admirable, if somewhat optimistic, goal. But I know I'll be laughing on the other side of my face when your bulb display is a local institution in your dotage. Just imagine: you yourself would be an actual institution – you'd love that. You'd be a date in the diary, a high day or even a holiday. Hyperbole aside, I think you'd actually be really good at that, as you're pretty efficient at hosting events in general. I crumble into a heap at the thought of more than three people for lunch, yet while I'm crumbling you're probably whipping up an apple crumble and making your table look rather wonderful at the same time. I forgot to tell you I've been inspired by your table linen – now there's a statement I never thought I'd make, but there it is. Walking down the King's Road the other day (be still, my beating heart... but how I miss the streets of London!), I noticed the little slice of heaven that is William Yeoward was having a sale, so nipped in and before I knew it, pounds had been spent on eight lilac cotton tablemats which at the time I thought might change my life and inspire me to invite seven for supper. But in the cold light of day I realised that it was probably more like a displacement activity – no change there. For as long as I can remember I've been putting off trying to give up procrastinating; I sound like a greetings card but it's true. I find myself wondering how much more I might have achieved if I had, say, actually read the whole of *Tess of the d'Urbervilles* at A level, rather than just the introduction and *Brodie's Notes*. The irony is that when I read it for the first time twenty years later, it turned out to be rather a gripping read. But you remember what it was like when we were seventeen – the things people told you to do were the things you definitely weren't going to do, at any price.

Table settings and sunshine turn my thoughts to Easter. For all my lack of adroitness at making a table look spit-spot, I do get very overexcited at the thought of rustling up a festive decoration or two. (Remember last year, when I realised my greatest achievement was the fact that my Halloween decorations actually made small children weep as they walked up the garden path? The life-size animatronic witch was a particular triumph.) So I'm rooting out the slightly bedraggled, stick-legged, almost fluffless tiny yellow chicks, and decorations for the Easter Tree – by the way, what *is* that all about? Did you ever have an Easter Tree as a child? In the words of George W. Bush, that is some weird ****.

For some reason, as a teenager I always wanted to make a Simnel cake. I remember tearing the annual Easter recipe article out of my mother's *Perfect Housewife* magazine and planning one day to feed my own family with it. As things have turned out, no one here will ever touch it either – I have to admit the effect of the whole marzipan–ball combo isn't really what you'd call mouthwatering. Do you have any ideas for a good Easter-ish teatime cake which anyone will actually eat? (I know the labrador will eat it, but that's not the point.)

My fridge, by the way, is looking satisfyingly full this morning. I know this, in your opinion, creates a state of happiness worthy of Snoopy at his most happy.

Gardener

Dear Gardener,

I can't say we ever had those kinds of magazine in our house. They are the kind of publication that my mother reviled. As she wrote in her book, it was either fish and chips or Fortnum & Mason for her – she found everything in between pretty unbearable. Bear in mind she modelled herself on Nancy Mitford. I'm afraid those magazines embody everything she simply couldn't abide – with tips and tools on how to do it all, to boot. She was, however, very tidy and an excellent cook. I'm afraid I am not the former and hopefully I am sometimes the latter. I actually rather like those articles – maybe I read in them hope of finding serenity – if I tidy my cupboard in colour-order or restack my herb shelf in the manner that Mary Berry has recommended, all will be well again. (I actually do like doing that sort of thing, so there you go!)

In the same vein of my mother's thinking, I think the fridge should always be very empty or very full: in-between is always disappointing.

The garden is indeed looking spring-like: our first daffs have appeared and I am waiting for the tulips – in fact you are right, I just can't wait! I am so excited. The tulip mix you ordered for me last year turned out to be brilliant. The peach-coloured ones really were stunning; although they reminded me of blancmange (a bad thing), they were a sight to behold. A friend of mine came round and took a bunch of them, and everybody loved them, so you can take credit for starting the craze for flouncy tulips. I actually love spring: we've got it all to look forward to. Spring food is also delicious. Lighter and fresher and, like the plants, greener in general.

Now about the cake. (I love cake as much as tulips.) Tulips and cake. Who knew? I could add them to my CV under Significant Interests. The point about an Easter cake in my mind is that it should not be chocolate. What?! Yes, it's true. One has scoffed so much chocolate on the day, the last thing anyone can face is a chocolate cake. I do know a rather delicious lemon and almond cake. I have added home-made lemon curd on top (so thick and scrumptious) and then scattered toasted pine nuts all over it. It is absolutely delicious. The pine nuts give it a Jerusalem angle (don't know why) and the lemon flavour makes it taste so fresh. It has a really Eastery feel to it and if you can only manage a tasting of it on Easter Sunday, it really is fantastic for breakfast with a cappuccino.

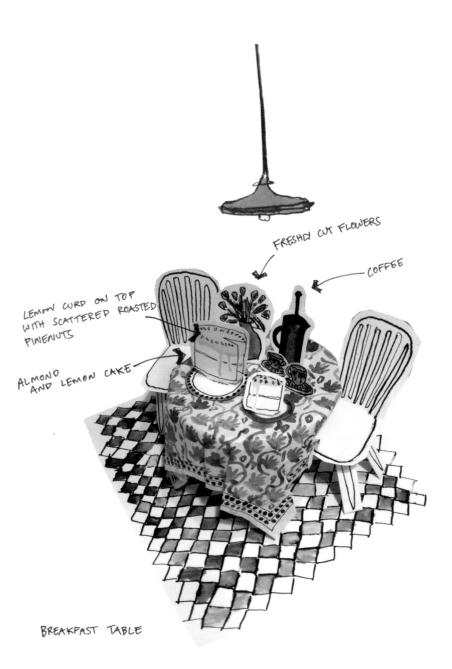

FRESHLY CUT FLOWERS

COFFEE

LEMON CURD ON TOP
WITH SCATTERED ROASTED
PINENUTS

ALMOND
AND LEMON CAKE

BREAKFAST TABLE

Lemon and almond cake with lemon curd and toasted pine nuts

SERVES 6

225g (8oz) unsalted butter

225g (8oz) caster sugar

225g (8oz) ground almonds

3 eggs

Zest of 2 lemons

Juice of 1 lemon

110g (4oz) plain flour

1 tsp baking powder

A pinch of salt

Use a 9 inch (23cm) loose-bottomed tart tin and grease with a bit of butter so the cake doesn't stick

For the lemon curd
(MAKES 450G, OR 16OZ – ABOUT A LARGE JARFUL)

2 large lemons
85g (3oz) unsalted butter
170g (6oz) granulated sugar
3 eggs, lightly beaten

Preheat the oven to 160°C. Mix the butter and sugar until pale and light. Stir in the ground almonds then gradually beat in the eggs. Fold in the lemon zest, lemon juice, flour, baking powder and salt. Spoon into the prepared tin and bake for 50 minutes.

To make the lemon curd for the topping, grate the zest of the lemons and squeeze out the juice. Put the lemon juice, butter, sugar and eggs into a heavy saucepan and stir constantly over a low heat until the mixture is thick. It takes quite a long time and can look like it's not working – it probably is so just be patient. Pass the mixture through a sieve and stir in the lemon zest. Leave to cool and smear generously over your cake. Toast your pine nuts (the most perilous part of the recipe) and scatter on top.

I know you are always worried about the children liking things, but they have normally eaten so much lunch and pudding that they are not interested in cake. It's really for the adults, and to put out a cake at teatime to celebrate the day. If you want to make something for them, make some Rice Krispie crackles to show them you care. Throw on some Mini Eggs and you look like you've made a massive effort. Otherwise, rustle up this chocolate biscuit cake – always a triumph – recipe below. Either way, perfect!

It seems to be a bit patronising to tell you how to make this cake when a five-year-old can do it, but I just wanted to remind you of it. I often serve it up in small pieces with coffee after a lunch, and I haven't met many who can resist it; even people you and I call 'competitive non-eaters' can't help but have a mouthful. So despite being a humble, very easy recipe, it is one that both adults and children like.

Chocolate biscuit cake

SERVES 8 (BUT WHEN CUT INTO SMALL PIECES IT SERVES A LARGE CROWD)

250g (8oz) plain biscuits (digestives or rich tea are good)
150g (5oz) milk chocolate broken up into pieces
150g (5oz) dark chocolate broken up into pieces
100g (3½ oz) unsalted butter
150g (5oz) golden syrup
60g (2oz) chopped nuts (optional)

Grease a 20cm square tin with some butter or use cling film to line the tin and leave some extra cling film hanging over the sides. Put the biscuits in a plastic bag and bash them into pieces using a rolling pin. Melt together the chocolate, butter and golden syrup – I just melt them in a pan on the top of the Aga. But as you are Aga-less, just melt them in a heatproof bowl set over a pan of simmering water.

Remove the bowl from the heat and stir in the broken biscuits and nuts, if you have used them. (If you like, you can add dried fruit e.g. apricots, raisins or cranberries – you'll need about 100g – but I think the original recipe goes down better with diners.)

Spoon the mixture into the tin and press down. Leave to cool, then put in the fridge for 1–2 hours to set. Turn out the cake and peel off the cling film. Cut up into pieces according to appetite.

While I am at it, I must include a great favourite recipe of mine for chocolate torte. My mother-in-law gave it to me. It is easy (phew) and great to serve up at a dinner party or family lunch – again everyone likes it, one size fits all, etc.

Easy chocolate torte

SERVES 8

200g (7oz) dark chocolate broken up into pieces
200g (7oz) melted unsalted butter
4 large eggs
100g (3½ oz) caster sugar
50g (1½ oz) light brown sugar
100g (3½ oz) ground almonds
Use an 8 inch (20cm) loose-bottomed tart tin and smear the whole
   tin with a bit of butter to prepare

Preheat the oven to 180°C. Melt together the chocolate and butter. While they are melting, separate the eggs. Mix the egg yolks and sugars together in a mixer or with an electric whisk. Let the melted chocolate and butter cool a little then stir into the eggs, followed by the almonds.

Whip up the egg whites until stiff. Using a metal spoon, fold the whites into the chocolate mixture. Scoop the mixture into the tin and put into the oven for 30–40 minutes.

The cake should be ready when it has a slightly crusty top – put a skewer in and see how clean it is when it comes out. You don't want the cake wet inside or too dry.

May the bunnies be with you,

Cook

Dear Cook,

I realise the irony of the fact that you rather like a read of those housewifery magazines now, whereas I'll avoid all similar make-yourself-the-perfect-domestic-goddess publications AS THEY JUST MAKE ME FEEL INADEQUATE. I get swamped by the imaginary speech bubbles saying #blessed #solucky and other absolutely unbearable outpourings of drivel. Whatever happened to sarcasm and irony? It seems to me that social media has stopped people making even just the teeniest little comment that might put a friend who's getting rather above herself, or just slightly smug, back firmly in their place. Now we have to be fake-honest the whole time. Or is it honest-fake? Whatever it is, I'm sure it's all getting out of control and that soon the world is going to be full of self-satisfied twits who dissolve at the first hint of criticism.

Easter eats: I read, digested, cooked, ate and digested. The lemon and almond cake was a stroke of genius – it was different, splendid and refreshing all at the same time. Everyone gobbled it up – every last teeny little pine nut. Seems to me that what stops me baking is sheer terror – everything looks so daunting when presented in a book, but instructions pinged over by a mate are somehow simply that: instructions. So I thank you.

I'm off to plant up some pots now. I picked up some fabulous scented geraniums from a little stall up by those traffic lights that are rarely ever green. People think that geraniums are tricky, but if you view them as bedding (anathema to all those who are very good at remembering to take cuttings each year), they really aren't that difficult at all. Just wait until the frosts have finished for the year, pop the geraniums in a good potting

ONE VARIETY IN ONE POT

POTS AT 'GREAT DIXTER'

compost in a container, group a few containers together, and bingo: a display. The key is to keep one variety in one pot, then do the grouping of pots, so you get that sumptuous effect of the collection of pots at Great Dixter – you must go if you haven't been yet this year.

Go before the daffs are over – they are really something: actual swathes of 'Emperor' daffodils actually swathing across the meadow.

Gardener

2

Mysterious anemones and the genius of asparagus

Dear Gardener,

My dog-walks over the years seem to have become nature-walks. As a born-and-bred city girl, I never pictured myself in a cagoule looking at acorns and blackberries but I do find myself walking along noticing certain things – a particularly beautiful blossom tree, some wonderful daisies, or a splendidly shaped, very green oak leaf. After twenty years of incarceration here, the country has had its benefits – the main upside for me being the joy of owning dogs and a good look at what's going on outside... I'll be on *Countryfile* next.

At the moment I keep seeing anemones on my walks, but when I look them up, one looks completely different from the other. Help. I hear some are small – how small? Do they come in different shapes as well as sizes – and are they Alpine flowers? I am not entirely sure what or where they can be squeezed into. In fact,

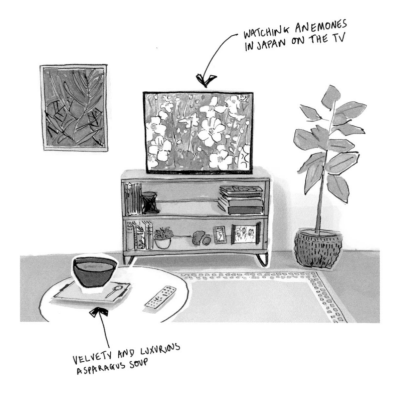

I am not entirely sure about anemones at all and seem to know nothing about them – do people actually grow anemones in their garden – and I am wondering if I should grow them. Are they another spring flower to add to the array, or do they come out a bit later? I'm sure I saw some in the woods last year, which means they must like shade – is my deduction correct? I've just remembered (this very second, as I write) watching someone like Monty Don on television at the Chelsea Flower Show discussing anemones and interviewing someone from Japan, so this means they must grow everywhere. Think I'm becoming the Poirot of Plantworld.

By the way, you mentioned asparagus the other day to me and asked what are my most favourite things about it. Well, the thing I like most about asparagus is that I never go off it – ever. I sometimes overuse certain ingredients or eat something just one time too many, but this never happens with asparagus: it's always delicious.

Many would say asparagus soup is a waste of the hallowed vegetable, but I think not. It is smooth, velvety and luxurious. If you have some slightly over-the-hill-looking specimens, these are perfect for the job, and it is very easy to make.

Velvet Asparagus Soup

SERVES 6

1 onion, chopped
3 or 4 bundles (or approx. 550g/20oz) of asparagus
Salt and pepper
1 litre vegetable or chicken stock
1 potato, chopped
Juice of half a lemon
30ml (1fl oz) double cream
A snipful of chives to finish off

Sweat the onion in a little oil and butter over a low heat, until softened. Cut off any woody ends from the asparagus, cut into pieces and add to the onion. Add some salt and pepper and leave to soften for about 5 minutes, but make sure nothing catches or sticks. Add the stock and the potato then leave to cook for about 20 minutes. Liquidise the soup; if you are a purist you may want to sieve it afterwards… Stir in the juice of half a lemon. Add the cream over a gentle heat then serve, sprinkled with the chives.

Other asparagus ideas

If you like croutons with asparagus soup, I would make small ones, about 1.5cm each side. Cut up some white bread into cubes, douse them in olive oil and salt then either fry them or put them on a tray in the oven at about 160°C. Another good addition are Parmesan biscuits – grate Parmesan on the inside of a biscuit ring on an oven tray and bake at 180°C for five minutes. This makes a sort of biscuit that you can float on top of the soup. It makes the soup truly delicious; I also think most soups benefit from a good half-a-lemon squeezed in.

Asparagus and taleggio cheese go together very well, too – you can just parboil the asparagus (that is, in and out of boiling water) then lay them in a baking tray and simply dot the cheese around the spears. For a more glamorous affair, put a square of puff pastry onto a baking tray and bake until light brown as per instructions on the packet. Place your asparagus spears on top, as if lined up like soldiers in a bed, and dot the taleggio liberally all over. Bake at 180°C for 10 minutes. This makes a lovely lunch with a green salad. Asparagus is also great in a salad, with smoked salmon and quails' eggs on a bed of mixed leaves – it's a lovely combination, and if you are a nutter add some pine nuts too. A simple olive oil-and-lemon dressing is all that is required here, with a sprinkle of salt and pepper.

I think asparagus risotto is one of the all-time greats. I know these days there are snazzier versions, with langoustine or pea and mint, but just asparagus on its own is refined and at the same time comforting. I think it's the Parmesan-and-butter-and-rice combo with the al dente asparagus that is so delicious. To elevate the supper, you can serve it with a roast chicken breast.

Asparagus risotto

SERVES 6

750ml (26fl oz) vegetable or chicken stock
450g (16oz) asparagus
55g (2oz) butter
1 tbsp olive oil
2 medium onions, finely chopped
350g (10½ oz) Arborio rice
200ml (7fl oz) white wine
80g (3oz) Parmesan cheese, grated
A knob of butter
Salt and pepper

Put your stock in a saucepan and gently heat it up. Get rid of any woody, stringy bits of the asparagus spears and chop up the rest into 2cm pieces. Put the tips to one side. Steam or boil the spears until al dente and just blanch the tips, by simmering them for 1–2 minutes.

Melt the butter and oil in a wide, heavy-bottomed saucepan and sauté the onions until soft and translucent (if you think it is getting at all burned you can add a dash of water). Add the rice and coat it with the onions and oil over a medium heat. Add the wine, a glug at a time – it will hiss – and let the alcohol waft through the kitchen. Now ladle in some stock and keep stirring your risotto. After 15–20 minutes it should be al dente. Now add your spears and keep stirring, after another 5 minutes add the tips of the asparagus – it probably needs another 5 minutes. Keep tasting – you want the rice to still have a bit of bite to it. Stir in your Parmesan and take off the heat. Add the knob of butter and leave the risotto for a couple of minutes with the lid on. Season with salt and pepper – *pronto*.

Cook

Dear Cook,

Try not to get Anemone Anxiety. The sweetest ones are the tiny blue or white starry flowers which you find in woodland. But buy your own – honestly, they can be squeezed into every pot. The corms (the anemone version of a bulb) are small and knobbly and look rather like wizened walnuts, which is how to distinguish them from daffodil bulbs (which look a bit like onions but are NOT for the kitchen) and from crocus bulbs (which look like small daffodil bulbs – simple).

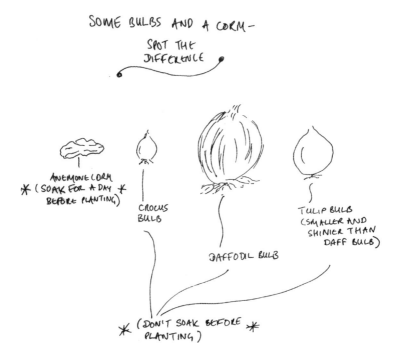

SOME BULBS AND A CORM –
SPOT THE DIFFERENCE

ANEMONE CORM
* (SOAK FOR A DAY *
BEFORE PLANTING)

CROCUS BULB

DAFFODIL BULB

TULIP BULB
(SMALLER AND SHINIER THAN DAFF BULB)

* (DON'T SOAK BEFORE *
PLANTING)

There is indeed a Japanese anemone – a lovely, tall-stemmed plant that looks great winding its way through the autumn border (so not just a spring flower). There's a gorgeous white one, 'Honorine Jobert', which works well in shadier spots, too. I can see where the confusion has arisen as there are loads of different varieties of anemone that don't look as if they should be related: *Anemone coronaria* is yet another type – this one is excellent as a cut flower in early summer so, once again, not just a spring flower. For your info, these get planted at the same time as tulip bulbs. Again, many to choose from – go for anything with 'De Caen' in the name as they are gorgeous, with velvety petals in rich, jewel-like colours. A must.

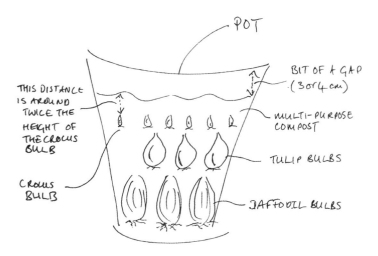

Thanks for the mouth-watering recipes, and also thanks for not asking me how to grow said spears: asparagus requires patience and, like many of us, a bed of its own. The key is not to harvest the spears in the first year – advice that I absolutely know you could not be trusted to follow. If you ask me again in a year's time, I'll know you're committed.

Gardener

3

The merits of bluebells and a salad Top Ten

Dear Gardener,

I love springtime and I gaze at bluebells in awe. The purpleness of them really is extraordinary. I drive past some near my house, all on a bank surrounded by trees, looking just amazing.

I know they are a wild flower but can one actually grow them? If you put some in a border would they simply take over? I am also rather puzzled about bluebell scent: do they actually have one? I see many bubble baths, body lotions and soaps that claim to be bluebell-scented. Search me if I know what that smells like.

Are white bluebells, well, bluebells? Just wondered…

Cook

Dear Cook,

You can indeed have bluebells – you must have bluebells! Make sure you buy the native ones, which are labelled as *Hyacinthoides non-scripta*. These are the common ones that do have a sweet scent, not the Spanish bluebell, which we need to avoid as it has a habit of swamping – and no scent: double trouble. Throw a handful of the common type under trees and then plant them as deep as you can – at least 4 inches – and you'll have drifts of blue (and white – yes, white are blue too) in your garden for ever.

As winter waves its last, hearty casseroles seem somewhat over the top and I'm longing for a change from the one-potters that have been seeing us through the season – I can't face another coq au vin. As you're known as the Salad Queen (even though you did actually award yourself that title), can you ping me over the salmon one you made us for lunch the other day? It wasn't smoked salmon, yet it was – I think.

Gardener

Dear Gardener,

Thanks for those tips – very useful. Gosh, bluebells for ever – that is a nice thought; and stick to the British type – dodgy advice right now, but I will go for it!

I did award myself that title and I think I deserve it as I do make a good salad. I can't claim that salad is real cooking. As far as I am concerned it's knowing what is delicious and what ingredients go together. I love salad, and winter ones just need to be a bit more filling in my opinion, but not necessarily hot. You can buy hot-smoked salmon fillets in most supermarkets and if you have them ready in the fridge at the beginning of the week they make a really hearty salad matched with some quinoa, an avocado, a bit of beetroot and some yoghurt smeared over the top. Quite often I put a whole goat's cheese in the oven and have it with salad, beetroot if I have it or oven-roasted tomatoes. Chicken salad is an obvious one, too, with ciabatta croutons and a bit of crispy Parma ham or bacon and some red peppers (just use the ones from a jar for ease). Walnuts, pears, apples and celery teamed with a lovely bit of cheddar for an old-fashioned Waldorf really hits the spot for me.

Here are some of my best ones and the ones that I love to eat:

Salad Top Ten

EACH SALAD SERVES 8, UNLESS I'VE SAID OTHERWISE

1. Three-bean salad with parsley, lemon juice and olive oil

I use this a lot as a 'side order' to a main salad. It's great for a buffet lunch; it just adds another texture. I like mine with a lot of onion and parsley but you can make yours with as little or as much of each as you like. The beauty of it lies in that it takes about 3 minutes to prepare.

2 tins 'mixed bean salad' or any two tins of beans
    (e.g. kidney, borlotti or cannellini)
1–2 red onions, finely chopped
Plenty (i.e. loads) of chopped fresh parsley

5 tbsp of good olive oil
3 tbsp of red wine vinegar
Salt and pepper

Firstly strain your tins of beans of all water and put them into a large
bowl. Next, chop up your onions finely – I just do thin semicircle pieces.
Then chop up a lot of parsley (100g or more) and mix it and the onions
in with your beans. Then put in your olive oil and vinegar, and season
with salt and pepper.

2. Feta, mango, orange and watercress salad with a lime and olive oil dressing

This really is delicious. It normally goes with my seared tuna and small
roast potatoes but you could have it with anything.

2 bags watercress salad, rocket or mixed baby leaves
3 avocados
2 mangoes
1 orange
1½ packets of feta cheese
6 spring onions, finely sliced
Coriander, finely chopped

For the dressing
5 tbsp olive oil
Juice of 2 limes
Salt and pepper

Put the watercress, rocket or leaves in a salad bowl. Slice the avocados
and add to the bowl, along with their whole stones – this stops the

avocado going brown (I'm sure most of you know this, but it really is a brilliant thing to know if you don't). Cut up your mangoes into small, bite-size pieces and add them to the bowl. Peel an orange and segment it, and de-pith each segment. Add these to the bowl along with the feta, cut up into squares. Slice your spring onions and scatter over the salad.

For the dressing, mix up the olive oil and lime juice, and season with the salt and pepper. Liberally sprinkle chopped coriander over the top of the salad. Ready to serve.

3. Niçoise salad

I think everyone thinks Niçoise is a bit boring now but I think it's a really useful one to remember. I prefer it with tinned tuna but I would understand if you preferred fresh, seared tuna steaks, and for a quick lunch with friends, served up with some delicious bread, it's unbeatable. You can add a tin of butter beans or a few strips of red pepper from a jar, and in spring languish some asparagus spears over the top.

450g (16oz) new potatoes (optional)
8 hardboiled eggs (everyone who likes egg really likes egg)
2 tins of tuna
A handful of olives
1 red onion, thinly sliced (optional)
200g (8oz) green beans, cooked al dente
4 Little Gem lettuces or 2 bags of mixed leaves of your choice

For the dressing
2 tsp Dijon mustard
3 tbsp white wine vinegar
8 tbsp olive oil
Juice of half a lemon
A pinch of sugar

Cook your potatoes in boiling water until tender then put to one side (you don't have to have the potatoes if you are in a hurry or on a diet). Hardboil your eggs (about 10 minutes) and thinly slice your red onion. Put all the salad ingredients together and try and make it look nice.

Mix up the dressing in a jam jar or cup and pour onto the salad. Eat with delicious bread.

4. Caesar salad

Again, I know this is an oldie and a bit obvious but the thing is, whenever I am with my children and their friends it is always what they order in a restaurant. If you make it at home, it really is all about the dressing.

2 Cos lettuces
125g (4oz) of raw spinach
4 chicken breasts (optional)
8 rashers of smoked streaky bacon, or Parma ham if you prefer
85 g (3oz) Parmesan shavings
Croutons, made from Ciabatta bread

For the dressing
4 tbsp of bought mayonnaise
3 anchovy fillets
2 garlic cloves
Juice of half a lemon
3 tbsp of olive oil
40g (1½ oz) Parmesan cheese, grated
Salt and pepper

In a large, flat salad bowl, rip up your lettuce and mix in the spinach. If you are having the chicken, put it into the oven and roast for 20–25 minutes or gently poach the breasts in some water in a covered saucepan for 20 minutes. Leave the cooked chicken to rest before cutting into strips. Cook your bacon or Parma ham until crispy. Break into pieces and scatter over the salad.

Whizz up all the dressing ingredients in a small mixer to a smooth paste – if it's a bit thick add a little cold water and mix again; I think the dressing should be on the thin side for Caesar salad, otherwise it can be gloopy. Season with salt and pepper. If you would like, you can add croutons made from ciabatta. Just cut up the bread into small squares and coat in olive oil and salt and put in the oven for about 8–10 minutes.

5. Snap-and-crackle tuna salad

This is such a delicious salad – it can be a main course or a starter. I have done it as a starter and then had Thai curry for the main course, which was a really good dinner party ensemble! I have also served it at my book club with side orders of chips. It is just so good…

SERVES 8 AS A STARTER

4 tuna steaks
4 tbsp miso paste
100g (3½ oz) sesame seeds
450g (16oz) frozen edamame beans
400g (14oz) radishes
400g (14oz) sugar snap peas or mangetout
Spring onions
20–30g (1oz) sushi ginger
Lots of coriander, chopped
1–2 handfuls crispy-fried shallot flakes (you can buy these online
    and they make a real difference to Asian salads – they just add
    another texture and another crunch)
Unsalted peanuts, smashed up in a pestle and mortar
Sesame oil and olive oil, for frying

For the dressing
3 tbsp soy sauce
2 tbsp fish sauce
Lime juice, to taste

To serve
1–2 tsp of wasabi paste
1 tub (200ml or 7oz) of crème fraîche

Completely smother one side of the tuna steaks with miso paste, using a knife or your fingers, then cover it with sesame seeds.

Now make the salad. Cook the edamame beans as per packet instructions and load them onto a platter. Cut up the radishes into circles and add to the edamame. Cook the mangetout briefly so that they are al dente and add them. Chop the spring onions, slice the ginger into slivers and throw those all in too.

Cook the tuna steaks in a frying pan with sesame oil and a bit of olive oil. Flash-fry them on both sides, leaving them to cook for about 1 minute (depending on thickness) on each side. You want them seared but pink on the inside; better to cook them less than more, as you can always shove them back on the heat for a few seconds. Slice the cooked tuna into long but fairly thick strips.

Put everything into a mound on each plate and add some of the crushed peanuts and crispy shallots. (If you are unable to get the shallots or the peanuts, do not fret – they are extras to make this salad more moreish but it will be really delicious anyway!) Scatter coriander over the whole salad (and use plenty).

Mix your wasabi into the crème fraîche and pass round the wasabi crème fraîche or put a dollop on each plate – whichever way you fancy.

6. Lentils, roast tomatoes, feta and fresh thyme salad with an olive oil, tangerine and mustard dressing

1 butternut squash or a packet of pre-cut butternut squash
500g (18oz) cherry tomatoes or 10 sundried tomatoes
Salt and pepper
200g (7oz) bacon lardons
400g (14oz) green beans or a mix of 200g (7oz) green beans and
  200g (7oz) mangetout
1 packet of feta cheese
1 bunch of fresh thyme
50g (2oz) rocket
2 tins of lentils or 2 sachets of ready-cooked lentils

For the dressing
3 tbsp olive oil
1 tsp grainy mustard
1 tbsp Greek yoghurt
1 tbsp runny honey
Juice of half a lemon
Juice of 1 tangerine

Cut your butternut squash into wedges (unless using pre-cut squash) and roast for 25 minutes at 160°C – if using fresh tomatoes, halfway through cooking put the tomatoes on top of the squash and season with salt and pepper. If you haven't got time, just use some sundried tomatoes but don't roast them with the squash – just cut them up. Fry your lardons until crispy. Cook your green beans or mangetout until al dente. Slice up your feta. Pick off the leaves from your thyme.

Spread the rocket over a serving plate or around the edge of it. In a bowl, mix together your lentils, lardons, beans or mangetout, tomatoes, squash and thyme. Mix all the dressing ingredients together. Add some dressing to the mixing bowl, then cover the rocket with the salad. Dot bits of feta all over and in the salad.

7. Warm goat's cheese, red pepper and pine nut salad

6 red peppers
3 flat round goat's cheeses (not the really soft type)
2 packets of mixed leaves
100g (3½ oz) pine nuts, toasted

For the dressing
6 tbsp olive oil
2 tbsp balsamic vinegar
½ tsp honey
½ tsp Dijon mustard

Put your peppers in the oven whole, to roast at 200°C for 20 minutes. Take them out and leave to cool down a bit while you bake the three goat's cheeses in the oven, at the same temperature, for about 10 minutes. Meanwhile, get your mixed leaves on a platter, cut your peppers into strips (I leave the skins on, I like them and I can't be doing with putting them in a plastic bag, etc) and scatter them over the lettuce.

Once the cheeses have puffed up, remove them from the oven and put them on the top of your lettuce and peppers. Scatter on your toasted pine nuts, mix up the dressing and pour over. Serve with a crusty baguette.

8. Mixed leaf, poached egg, Parma ham and pomegranate salad

SERVES 1 GENEROUSLY

This is a good hangover salad, when the lure of bacon and eggs is very tempting.

2 eggs
100g (3½ oz) mixed leaves (1 medium-sized bag)
4 slices Parma ham, roasted in the oven until crispy
A handful of pomegranate seeds
Just a few toasted pine nuts (optional – but they make me feel
   healthy so I add them to everything)

I think this is the best way to make a good poached egg: boil some water in a pan, put in a drop of vinegar if you like the taste (it doesn't help the cooking of the egg), crack your egg into a mug. Swirl your water in the saucepan then drop the egg in. Leave for one minute then leave off the heat for another 2 minutes. Remove with a slotted spoon.

Put your poached eggs on top of your salad leaves with the roasted Parma ham and – yes, you guessed it – the pomegranate seeds and toasted pine nuts.

9. Tomato, mozzarella and avocado salad

(INCLUDED AS SO MANY – INCLUDING RESTAURANTS – GET THIS WRONG)

I know this is *so* easy but it's important to get it right. I learnt to make it in Italy with a friend of my mother's who owned three restaurants and is Italian, so it must be right. Right or wrong, it's delicious.

8 tomatoes
3 avocados
3 packets of mozzarella (buffalo if possible, or the best you can get)
Lots of basil leaves
Lashings of olive oil
Salt

Slice your tomatoes into rounds and cut your avocado into fan slices. Simply arrange on a plate with your mozzarella and TEAR (do not cut up) the basil leaves over the top. Pour over the olive oil and season with the salt.

10. Duck breast, melon, mint and lamb's lettuce salad with pomegranate seeds

4 duck breasts

400g (14oz) broccoli

One cantaloupe melon (or any melon you fancy)

1 or 2 red chillies, deseeded and finely diced

2 packets (200g or 7oz) lamb's lettuce, or for a more peppery taste
  use rocket

1 packet of pomegranate seeds

20g (1oz) mint leaves

For the dressing

Juice of two limes

2 tbsp light soy sauce

2 tbsp fish sauce

A few grinds of black pepper

Olive oil

Preheat the oven to 180°C. Score the skin of your duck breasts then pan-fry them skin-side down for about 8 minutes. Finish off in the oven for about 10 minutes – ideally the duck should be pink in the middle. Leave to rest until cool-ish, then cut into slices.

Cook your broccoli until al dente and put to one side. Chop up your melon into bite-size pieces. Place your lamb's lettuce or rocket in a flat salad dish and scatter with the duck, broccoli, melon, chilli and pomegranate seeds. Tear – do not cut – the mint leaves over the top. Dress your salad and enjoy.

By the way, I would like to grow some lettuces as it seems churlish not to and you said they were very easy... I'm wondering if there is a way of growing them in smaller quantities? It's just as with some of the vegetables: they all rather come at once, and although a salad fanatic, even I cannot eat six a day. I know you are sighing right now, saying to yourself, 'Just plant fewer,' so I will rephrase: how many should one plant at a time, bearing in mind it is one family eating them, and could one do a sort of crop rotation, i.e. plant four on Monday and then another four on the Friday of that week, so that they are staggered and therefore will all be eaten?

Cook

Dear Cook,

Perfect. I have no problem with supply of salad leaves: we have grown the most marvellous lettuces: 'Merveille de Quatre Saisons' and 'Black Seeded Simpson' were, I swear, the easiest things to grow EVER. I popped the seeds in a pot, watered them when I remembered and then watered them again, and they turned into the biggest, fattest, lushest, leafiest bounty you ever did see. Plant them. Regarding numbers, again it's really a question of common sense – sow a row every couple of weeks. And that's all there is to it.

Gardener

4

Herbs and handsome hydrangeas

Dear Gardener,

I like to have hydrangeas in pots. Is this allowed in Gardener's world? There is a lot of talk about putting them in lime soil and planting in the shade but to be honest I have just bunged mine in pots with compost. They are now getting quite tall and leggy. I think my garden is really held together by the hydrangeas. They make it rather majestic in my view and I am generally delighted with them. You even commented when you came round that it looked good so I must be doing something right. As you know, I had my birthday party in the garden and everyone was complimenting it. Ha! My mother-in-law told me that this year I should grass over my flowerbeds (due to laziness on weeding front) but I am glad I ignored her comment now. It really is looking good, and what's a few weeds among friends?

Right, back to hydrangeas: should I now plant them in the flower bed and replace my pots with smaller ones? Plus (I told you I know nothing about gardening), do they go blue after being pink? Is the pink strangled out of them by the blue? I have to say

my current ones look magnificent and they really are a brilliant plant. On a still summer night when they are in their pots on the terrace they almost look surreal – they are so ultra-bright I feel like I'm in a technicolour 1950s blockbuster, and that makes me feel very cheerful, which is good. I'm trying to keep the blue hydrangeas blue, but the colour-changer acid thing I bought doesn't appear to be working as my whole garden seems to be variations of purple – it's a sort of mauve work of art. The purple revolution going on reminds me that I really need some good mid- to late-summer (July and August) colours in my borders and I suppose that means I should plant some this October. Any suggestions?

Cook

Dear Cook,

You can have whatever you like in pots – just follow the rule of thumb that if the plant doesn't do very well, take it out and don't plant it in a pot again. Hydrangeas will be fine as long as there's enough room for their roots, and that the pots are kept irrigated and out of blasting sunlight, so yours definitely should go out into the main beds now. The colour is due to acidity of soil – Google it – but essentially if you like blue you need to make the soil more acid: acid mulch is a way to do this if you can't be bothered to replace the soil completely. The enormous shower-cap blooms of Hydrangea 'Annabelle' have been all the rage for some time now: the white/lime-green flowers equal easy instant chic, a go-to solution for instant stylishness which I admit I've employed rather a lot over the years. They do look magnificent as they nod grandly over all they survey. This has made me remember what jolly good do-ers hydrangeas are. My current favourite is 'Moritzburg', which has big, fat mopheads of blooms in a very usual pink, but this pink then fades to exquisite purples and limes and deep reds which look totally at home in an autumnal vase in the parallel universe where I have time to cut flowers and bring them in to the house. Before you ask, 'do-er' is one of those gardening non-technical, non-specific terms which, when you employ them, make you feel like you truly are a member of a rather special community. Hardy geraniums and gauras (tall, wispy plants whose straggliness is mitigated by their tiny pink or white stars of flowers which go on ... and on ... and on) are often called 'good do-ers' – it means they're bulletproof. You can plant them quite roughly and without too much – or indeed any – skill, and they'll come back year after year after year, spreading or self-seeding as the whim takes them.

I can sense your eyes glazing over... Why not de-pot the hydrangeas and put herbs in the pots instead? Then you can have the pots near the kitchen and *voilà* – no having to venture too far when it's chucking it down outside.

Gardener

Dear Gardener,

I shall follow your tips... By the way, which herbs are best suited to outside pots? Can I grow any on a windowsill? Actually, ignore that – I haven't got a windowsill. Also, what is the point of buying a growing herb from a supermarket – because, as we know, they don't actually carry on growing? However well I follow the instructions ('place in a saucer and water, but do not over-water', etc) they just straggle and become a home for tiny flies.

One of the great herbs has to be rosemary – not necessarily to eat, but to smell and just look at. It seems very robust and I don't have to pay it much attention and it still grows.

I think my best herb, though, is parsley. It is just SO useful; it's adaptable and lends itself to many different dishes, and it doesn't lose its colour – but I have found it very challenging to grow. I think I am the only person I know who still makes hot ham with parsley sauce – a very comforting dish indeed. Do you remember Parsley the lion? He was my favourite character in *The Herbs* TV series back in prehistoric times.

Cook

Dear Cook

If it's of any reassurance, I have the same problem as you do with the growing herbs that you buy from supermarkets. Part of the problem is that it isn't just one basil plant, for example – it's a dozen or so seeds that have been forced to grow quickly, and they simply haven't had the right start to their lives to grow into big bushy plants. Basil's not great outside in our climate, but parsley and coriander are easily grown from seed. Plant a few (in separate lines so you can remember what they are when they are just tiny shoots) along the edges of your raised veg beds: they'll make a pretty frilly frame, and they respond really well to being cut – as if by magic they grow again, as long as you don't shear them off completely. Carry on cutting them – avoid letting them flower as they'll then go to seed and we all know what that infers. But I know there's no danger of your letting them get out of control – I've noticed that it's all about the flavour with a lot of your meals. I know that's going to elicit a 'Duhh' from you, but what

I mean is that you really do know your herbs and what they'll do to a dish.

You could also plant herbs around the edge of the pot. Rosemary is happiest outside and can go in a pot, so if you think of it as a flower arrangement, you'd use rosemary as the backbone and then put in things like sage, chives and thyme around it. (A small fact here: chives are related to alliums, as both are members of the onion family.)

Yes, I remember *The Herbs* – with Dill the dog and Lady Rosemary! Now that was a clever way of including a bit of gardening education. I'm sure we never appreciated the underlying themes in children's TV when we were tiny. I showed an episode of *Camberwick Green* to my sister's children when they were all staying last weekend. I'd gaily offered to do the morning stint, thinking with rose-tinted glasses that it would all be a complete breeze – I hadn't reckoned with the fact that they'd both be up at 5 a.m. – Oh My God, that brought back the actual horror of the relentless cycle of early mornings that toddlers so seem to love. Nobody tells you before you have babies that you will spend months and even years feeling like a complete zombie. I can't watch zombie films now, as when I see the walking dead it reminds me too much of me a few years ago.

Anyway, I realised during that dawn screening of desperation, apart from the fact that the picture was, I quote, 'all wiggly', that the episode had the central theme of the villagers campaigning against the installation of an electricity substation on the green of Camberwick. I was impressed.

G was never a fan though – he was a *Thomas the Tank Engine* afficionado, and I remember all too clearly the complete and utter relief when he would become immersed in the Island of Sodor. He was such a good baby, but all I can remember is feeling guilty that I wasn't doing the right thing – if he played by himself, I worried I should be interacting with him; but if I was interacting with him I'd worry that I should be letting him play by himself. It's a wonder we aren't all still truly bonkers, as I reckon motherhood does slightly make you temporarily insane.

Gardener

Dear Gardener

Ah yes... Those were tricky times, with tiny toddlers showing signs of infuriating, irrational behaviour. I think what gets us all through is that they are so adorable and endearing when they are being good! My son absolutely loved *Thomas the Tank Engine* too. I think I must have been utterly insane or very depressed at that stage in life. When I watched it with K I wasn't so much struck with the brilliance of Percy's or James's engines, but rather with the weather in Sodor. It was always sunny – literally, it was a nice day EVERY day. I found this grossly unfair when I looked outside at the drizzle on a dark November afternoon.

Anyway, I digress as usual. Here is what I would do with a bit of rosemary.

Individual feta, red onion, rosemary and thyme soufflés

SERVES 6

2 tbsp oil
50g (1½ oz) butter
2 small red onions, finely chopped
1 tbsp finely chopped rosemary
1 tbsp chopped thyme
30g (1oz) plain flour
¼ tsp mustard powder
A pinch of cayenne pepper
220ml (8fl oz) of milk
170g (6oz) feta cheese, crumbled
3 eggs, separated
Salt and pepper
Dry white breadcrumbs – enough to stick to the sides of each
    ramekin

I think soufflés are made out to be much more difficult than they actually are. You can even make them in advance and put them in the fridge for the day if you want. I don't mean to belittle the soufflé, but give it a go and I think you will agree with me.

Preheat the oven to 200°C. Next heat up some oil and 20g (½ oz) butter, add the onions and herbs, and sweat until the onions are soft but not coloured. In another pan, melt 40g (1½ oz) butter and brush the inside of the ramekins with it, then dust each ramekin with breadcrumbs so that they stick to the sides. Next melt the last 40g (1½ oz) of butter and stir in the flour, mustard powder and cayenne pepper – cook this for 45 seconds then blend in the milk and stir for about 2 minutes until the mix is very thick and leaves the sides of the pan. Remove from the heat. Next stir in the feta, egg yolks and onion mix. Season carefully with the salt and pepper – don't forget the feta is pretty salty in its own right. Next whisk the egg whites until stiff but not dry. Stir a bit into the cheese mix to loosen it, then fold in the remainder. Spoon into ramekins until about two-thirds full and run a knife around the top of the mixture on each ramekin; this should give a top hat appearance to the baked soufflé.

Put the ramekins onto a baking sheet and put in the oven for 15 minutes, then give them a shake and if you detect a wobbly, liquidy bit in the middle put them back in the oven for another 5 minutes.

These are delicious and a great starter – and don't forget you can prepare them in the morning and leave them in the fridge until you need them, and then cook them in the evening.

Cook

5

A bulb Top Ten and a 1970s curry

Dear Cook

I meant to say to you I thought the garden looked fabulous at your party – it was ingenious of Daisy to order miles of fairy lights; so, quickly, it looked so magical. I'm so sorry I was late arriving and late with the borage, which did look a bit sorry for itself at the beginning, but as soon as it hit the G&Ts it revived remarkably. You wouldn't have thought gin would have the same effect on plants as it does at 6 p.m. on a grey evening in the country, would you? That doesn't mean I'm suggesting it as a pick-me-up when flowers are wilting in a vase, but I do know that a sugar-rush of lemonade works well in that department if things are looking a bit limp.

Actually, though the garden looked great, in the cold light of day there are loads of gaps that you need to fill in if you want some colour next year. I promised to remind you so here it is: IT'S BULB ORDERING TIME, so why don't you earmark six of those massive holes where the hydrangeas used to be and order bulbs which will take you through (gardener term there) from January to May, and a little bit beyond that if you're lucky.

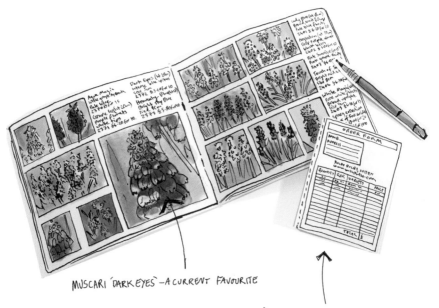

MUSCARI 'DARK EYES' — A CURRENT FAVOURITE

IT'S BULB ORDERING TIME!

Bulb Top Ten

(Halt your inner pedant: I'm including corms and tubers here – these all get planted at the same time, in late October into November.)

1. Blue and white anemones
Look for *Anemone nemerosa* and *Anemone blanda*.

2. Bluebells
Hyacinthoides non-scripta.

3. Snowdrops
The Latin name is *Galanthus*. Try any you like the look of, but £-alert here: some snowdrops might be £1 while others are £100. And if you get addicted to them, you will become known as a galanthophile. Really.

4. Crocus
I rather like *Crocus tommasinianus*, which is pale blue-mauve – bright enough to make you stop in your tracks when it appears as a blanket on a late-winter lawn, subtle enough to make you feel sad when they get flattened by the dog.

5. Muscari
These are the beautiful little grape hyacinths, usually in shades of blue: a current favourite of mine is 'Dark Eyes'. These naturalise, which means multiply – so plant five and after a few years you'll have twenty.

6. Iris

The mini ones are gorgeous. Plant these where you can see them; when skies are grey and the mood is low, a pot outside the door with the purples and blues of Iris 'George' and Iris 'Cantab' will make you glad you bothered.

7. Narcissus

Tall daffodils, tiny daffodils, big, yellow shouty ones and delicate, little primrose-coloured ones. This year I have planted 'Pistachio', 'Tickled Pinkeen' and 'Full Throttle'. I've never grown any of these before so the jury's out on the eventual effect next spring.

8. Camassia

These look a tiny bit like enormous bluebells, the really blue ones especially. Plant many, many of them (at least nine) in clumps in the grass – then don't mow the shoots as they start popping up in early spring. *Camassia cusickii* is the one to look for. If you want to mow, don't plant them in the grass obvs.

9. Tulips

Choose any you like and ring the changes every year, as they can't be relied upon to reappear annually. Go for a hot mix of deep reds, burgundies, purples and oranges ('Recreado', 'Violet Beauty', 'Ronaldo', 'Malaika') and follow it up the year after with shades of white and cream ('Flaming Purissima', 'Hakuun', 'Diana', 'White Triumphator') with the difference being in the shape of the flower itself. This is actually rather impressive, especially if you pop in a bit of peachy-pink 'Sweet Impression' if it's all getting a bit virginal...

Followed by MASSES of...

10. Alliums (purple drumsticks)

...though you probably need to hold back on the massed allium 'Purple Sensation' as they've been *le dernier cri* for so long that they're now rather becoming like Farrow & Ball – guaranteed tasteful purchase which is now everywhere and therefore in danger of being bland. Who'd have thought it? Try the larger ones – 'Globemaster', 'Gladiator' and 'Giganteum'; and the madder ones – 'Hair' speaks for itself, whilst 'Schubertii' is one big static firework of a plant.

Have to go now: by the smell of it, the M&S *frites* are way past crispy. Cheerios for lunch, sausages and chips for tea – it really is the end of the summer hols. What can I give the teen and pre-teen, Jack Sprat and his wife? One will eat carrots, one will eat tomatoes. Not the other way round, though. The same goes for green beans and mangetout, broccoli and cauliflower, and the two separate layers of shepherd's pie.

Gardener

Dear Gardener,

Thanks for all those tips – you are marvellous. I had a friend staying in the summer and she was perusing your notes on what bulbs to buy. She was engrossed and I think she even quickly took a picture with her phone when she thought I wasn't looking! So you see, everyone really does appreciate and value your advice, and uses it!

I really think you are overthinking your children's food selections. If you just think around the problem, you do baked potatoes rather than chips, which is a healthy meal in itself. If you make them ham-and-cheese toasties with a green salad; the one who doesn't want bread can just have salad with – you've got it – ham and cheese. It's a bit like me saying I'm scared of planting a bulb: don't be scared of food. It's just food. I think the more you pander to children's likes and dislikes, the more you will find yourself on the road to kitchen hell. Let them decide what they like from what you have put out.

Right, lecture over, and sorry I have not got a magical recipe that all toddlers, teens and adults like! Anyway, I digress into psychology. I do have, however, a foolproof chicken curry recipe. Jack Sprat and his wife could have either rice or curry on its own but you have made just one dish and therefore cut down on time and stress.

Foolproof chicken curry

SERVES 6

This is a recipe that really has no preparation or pretentions. It really is a 1970s classic, mostly based on a Delia Smith recipe. Her recipes were second nature to most of us during the 1980s; I don't think I know anyone who hasn't used her *Summer* and *Winter Collection*. It was our bible when it came to entertaining. In fact, I still use both books often. This is a curry made with dry spices and curry powder so you really can do it out of the store cupboard.

4 chicken breasts (skin off) and cut into bite-size pieces or 600g (21oz) leftover cooked chicken.
2 onions, chopped
2 garlic cloves, chopped
2 tsp ground ginger (or 1 inch of fresh root ginger peeled and finely chopped)
2 tsp paprika
2 tsp ground cumin
4 cardamom pods
1 tbsp medium curry powder
80g (3oz) ground almonds
400g (14oz) tin of coconut milk
400g (14oz) tin of tomatoes
2 tbsp olive or sunflower oil
200ml (7fl oz) chicken stock or plain boiled water
Salt and pepper
Squeeze of lemon or lime juice

Chop up your chicken into chunks or bite-size pieces and then brown them over a medium heat in a little olive oil for a few minutes. Set aside. In the pan fry the onions until soft and then add garlic and ginger. Add all the dry spices and fry for one minute. Put all of the onions and spices into a mini processor and add your almonds. Add a tablespoon of the boiled water or stock to thin it a bit. Next take a large, flat casserole dish or saucepan and heat a tablespoon of oil; add the spice paste and browned chicken.* Stir round for a minute and before it starts sticking add the coconut milk and a tin of tomatoes (I like to put mine in the mini processor so it is smooth). Then add salt and pepper to taste. If it is too thick add some of the water or stock. Cook for half an hour on a low to medium heat. Finish with some lemon or lime juice.

The point is this is a really easy recipe, but to make it a bit more snazzy chop some fresh coriander to go on top, serve it with a yoghurt and cucumber raita (see below) and put some poppadums on the table, too. The little extras make a REAL difference. Serve with rice and mango chutney. YUM.

* If using leftover chicken put in the sauce towards the end of the cooking time.

Cucumber and herb raita

25g (1oz) mint
25g (1oz) coriander
1 red onion
2 green deseeded chillies
1 tsp salt
1 tsp sugar
Juice of 1–2 lemons (to taste)
300g (10½ oz) natural yoghurt
Half a cucumber, grated

In a small food processor, whizz up the mint, coriander, onion, chillies, salt, sugar and lemon juice. Stir the mixture into the yoghurt along with the grated cucumber.

When you put it like this it looks so easy, and then it turns out it actually *is* easy. Both children love it, and the poppadums are a brilliant way of making them think it's all rather a treat. I do think you're being a bit harsh, though: I firmly believe some things are Nature Not Nurture. How is it that G's idea of the perfect day is a visit to the fishmonger's and selecting the most unidentifiable wet thing, whilst C gags at the mere mention of salmon? I believe you will not have the answer to that conundrum, my very dear friend.

Dear Gardener,

Here's a good Thai curry but it involves making a paste, which isn't that time-consuming, but if you are tired just use a shop-bought paste – it's still a great dish.

A good Thai curry

SERVES 4

1½ tbsp palm sugar

2 tbsp fish sauce

750ml (26fl oz) coconut milk

4 chicken breasts or boneless thighs, skin off and cut into 2cm
  pieces

3 kaffir lime leaves

3 red chillies

Thai basil leaves or coriander

Juice of 2 limes

More fish sauce, to taste

For the curry paste

6 dried long red chillies, deseeded, soaked and drained

A pinch of salt

1 tsp chopped coriander stems

1½ tbsp fresh ginger

1 tbsp chopped lemongrass

3 tbsp chopped shallots

2 tbsp chopped garlic

Half a nutmeg, pounded or grated

4 tbsp of peanuts

Make the curry paste by grinding all the ingredients together in a large pestle and mortar or small food processor, adding the peanuts at the end. (You can freeze this paste in ice-cube trays then put the cubes into bags so you have them at the ready. I must admit I have never done this, but it is on my to-do list!)

Over a medium to low heat, fry the curry paste for about one minute until it becomes aromatic. Add the palm sugar and some fish sauce, to taste. Pour in the coconut milk and bring to a simmer. Add the chicken, lime leaves and red chillies, then gently simmer till the chicken is cooked through.

If you want the sauce a bit thicker, take out the cooked chicken and let the liquid bubble until it has reduced it; or, in a mug, make a paste with a teaspoon of cornflour and a little of the sauce, and stir back into the sauce, adding the chicken back in once the sauce is to your liking.

Stir in the Thai basil and/or coriander, the lime juice, season with salt and pepper and serve with rice.

Cook

6

Veg beds and soft fruit

Dear Gardener,

I am writing to question the merits of a kitchen garden. It is the quintessential 'good life' hobby: grow your own and you will feed yourself, reduce your carbon footprint and generally be a very good egg indeed. You will probably never have to go to a supermarket again.

I have a sneaking suspicion that there is a lot of extra veg floating around country villages during the month of August. A friend of my sister's had a good idea: have a container outside the village hall, put all your extra potatoes in and take for yourself what you don't have (i.e. some of your neighbour's leeks). You see, the truth is most people can't eat all the vegetables they grow. I think you have to really plan what you actually are going to eat. After eight years of growing vegetables in my boxes (which you designed – thank you), I have got it down to a tee. I grow onions and – well, onions. Onions last for ages – you can store them for months – and we do actually eat them. But here is the thing: while I only grow onions, I still love the look of my boxes and I love the look of growing my own, so along with my onions I grow some flowers – sweet peas, unusually large sunflowers. And I have a fruit

The actual harvest

box; I am very happy with my rhubarb, my gooseberries and even my blackcurrants. Herein lies another problem, though: my redcurrants. During May they are beginning to ripen. I watch with anticipation as they slowly turn. Yet I am not the only one watching. The thrushes, the sparrows and the magpies are like the MI5 Special Branch of my garden. As soon as the berries turn – and I mean as soon as – they swoop down and get 'em… Gone. Once again I have lost the competition: wings vs legs – and the wings get it every time. (NB don't tell me to get a net as they always get holes and birds get caught up in them, which I can't stand.)

So am I sad? Not gutted, actually. The truth is I really don't like summer pudding; soggy bread and wet fruit has never been my thing, even if it is smeared with double cream. I could make redcurrant jelly but there are not quite enough berries. Shall I ditch the redcurrants?

My bottom-line question is: Gardener, what is in your dream veg bed, and why?

Cook

Dear Cook

It's funny you should say that about summer pudding – it's something we pretend to like when we're in that impressing-people-with-our-sophistication stage (rather like kedgeree). I reckon you have to hit forty before you can say 'wet bread and sour fruit – REALLY?' Come to think about it, a child would say that, too. I reckon, actually, that there's a window between the age of nineteen and thirty-six where people fake summer-pud-love. And yes, it was on the menu at my wedding – do you think that could have been an omen? It is definitely one of those dishes that gives British cookery a bad name On The Continent. Can you imagine serving up a wedge of purple-stained sodden *pain* to an Italian?

So perhaps the redcurrants are a waste of your *tempo* – the birds will be annoyed, but you can use the space to grow what you know you'll eat. Lettuces, cut-and-come-again salads, parsley, perpetual spinach – these all do go down a storm here with both of my children, especially if the seeds have been sown and grown by ourselves. Teenagers are more interested in this than the littlest – which proves my point that you can't force children to love gardening: they'll do it when they discover it for themselves. So all those simply explained sections in the seed catalogues that are aimed at toddlers: I send them the teenagers' way. They get rather absorbed.

Here's to green leaves and dream veg. But… having said all that, there must be SOME berry recipe which will use up all the ones you've grown, without requiring lorry-loads of the things? Berries always look so photogenic in recipe photos, but more often than not the anticipation is a little better than the event.

Gardener

HURST GREEN SHAFT PEA
– GROW PEAS UP SOMETHING

PERPETUAL SPINACH
(IT DOES WHAT IT
SAYS ON THE TIN)

ITALIAN PARSLEY
KEEP CUTTING IT TO USE,
AND IT WILL KEEP
COMING BACK

BLACK–SEEDED SIMPSON LETTUCE
– CRISP AND SWEET

EDGE TIMBER
WITH SOME COPPER
TAPE TO DETER SLUGS

USE PLANKS OR NEW SLEEPERS,
NEVER RECLAIMED SLEEPERS AS
THEY ARE FULL OF CREOSOTE

Dear Gardener,

I'm afraid I cannot claim the following to be a recipe, as such, but I must admit I have got a few people hooked on it – and it involves raspberries, not redcurrants. (Incidentally an acquaintance of mine does make redcurrant jelly but she puts a label on it saying 'Mrs Smith's [not real name] Jelly'. I find this peculiar as a) she hates her husband so why advertise yourself as his wife? And b) it's smug and annoying and we do not live in the 1950s any more.)

I really have got my breakfast down to a tee. It is the 'hot berry breakfast' – and I'm ashamed to admit it is nothing to do with my unbountiful berry harvest. I buy frozen raspberries and I heat up a bowlful of them every morning in the microwave (you could do it in a pan if without microwave), then I add Greek yoghurt, honey and some flaked almonds. My husband adds Grape-Nuts – obviously you can have granola, too, but this makes it a tad more fattening. I feel I have transformed many of my friends' breakfasts and it is so good and warming and filling AND HEALTHY. I must insist you try it. Now who is smug and annoying?

A really good pudding is a lemon roulade with raspberries. I think roulades, like soufflés, are seen as something tricky to make. They are not, and as they are supposed to look cracked when served it means you can't really go wrong.

Lemon roulade with raspberries

SERVES 6–8

For the sponge

5 large eggs, separated
140g (5oz) caster sugar
Grated zest of 2 lemons
Juice of 1 lemon
60g (2oz) ground almonds
Sieved icing sugar, for dusting (optional)

For the filling

300ml (11fl oz) double cream, whipped
60g (2oz) caster sugar
450g (16oz) raspberries

Preheat the oven to 180°C and find a 30 x 35cm (12 x 13 inch) tin. Brush the tin with melted butter and line with baking parchment so the paper sticks to the tin. You can brush butter on top of the paper, too, for easy removal later on.

Using a handheld electric mixer, whisk together the egg yolks and sugar – the mix should be quite thick and pale. Stir in the lemon rind and juice along with the ground almonds.

In another, very clean, bowl, whisk your whites until they are stiff and you can turn the bowl upside down above you without them falling on your head. Then, using a metal spoon, fold the whites into the egg yolk mix. Pour the batter into the tin, level the top and bake in the oven for 20 minutes. It should be firm and maybe even slightly cracked. Leave to cool in the tin, covered with a damp tea towel.

Stir your caster sugar into your whipped cream to sweeten it. Turn your cooled roulade upside down onto the tea towel and peel off the baking parchment. Spread your cream over the sponge and roll it up. I am messy so this sometimes looks, well, messy. The other day I grated white chocolate on top of the roulade, which made it look more professional. My mother-in-law came in while I was doing it and thought I was covering it with Parmesan! Dot raspberries around, if you fancy; you can dust it with more sieved icing sugar, too.

Cook

Dear Cook

Roulade sounds DELICIOUS and the berry breakfast is definitely on my agenda. But Grape-Nuts? I didn't know they still existed and so went out and tracked some down. I have to say, I'd forgotten how jaw-ache-inducing Grape-Nuts really are. Good for anyone on a diet, I suppose, as it takes a good five minutes to get around every mouthful. I felt very vintage eating them; maybe they could be washed down with a bottle of ginger beer?

I roared when I read about Mrs Smith's (not her real name) Jelly. When I first told London friends that we were moving to the country, they were aghast, telling me I'd have to go to coffee mornings and make muffins. Sure enough, shortly after arriving in the middle of nowhere, I found myself as a coffee-morning guest in a kitchen with cupboards painted in Elephant's Bum and Mouse's Fart and similar. The topics of conversation, all passively-aggressively competitive in an unsaid way, mainly involved babies' milestones (weaning, talking, schools, poos – competitive poos might have been the cause of some mild post-natal depression). But what most filled me with horror was what was on the granite worktops. (Another source of competition at that time was who had the best granite for their worktops – I promise you that this was an actual discussion I heard one day, when people even brought their individual granite samples. If any of you guys are reading this, you know who you are and you should be ashamed of yourselves.) Anyway, what should be proudly displayed there on the speckled-black surface but several baskets of home-made (obvs) muffins, each proudly sporting a hand-calligraphed label of 'Chocolate', 'Vanilla', and, rather thrillingly, 'Chocolate and Vanilla'. It scarred me for life.

Gardener

Dear Gardener,

I must say, I have to agree with you on all your points – and I bet those muffins were shop-bought, anyway. It all really begs the question, 'What is wrong with everybody?' It seems that highly educated women who should be doing and talking about interesting things have instead found themselves playing the main part in a suburban soap opera. I am REALLY glad the coffee-morning era is over for us.

By the way, I meant to tell you that I've really got into autumn this year – firstly by noticing the acorns on my dog-walks. There are loads this year and I am really enjoying crunching them underfoot – a very satisfying experience. I have also had two absolutely delicious pears. So...? I hear you say, but this really is quite a mean feat. I remember Eddie Izzard once making a very good pear observation. He described how he bought them, put

them in the fruit bowl, gazed at them knowing that they were too hard to eat so left them alone, only to find two mornings later that they were too soft, even almost furry. He illustrates my point that finding a ripe pear, a properly ripe one, is an absolute result.

I was visiting my friend in Hampshire last week and she's got two pear trees. They are flat against a rather nice brick wall. How tricky are they to grow? And does it take years for them to bear fruit? They really are one of my favourite ingredients.

Cook

Dear Cook

The art of the espalier – for that's what's been done to those pears – is fairly simple to get a grip on but it does require a certain amount of patience, which is why there's a boom at the moment in nurseries supplying ready-grown versions.

Essentially, with an espalier you can choose what pattern you want the tree to grow in. You can have it like this:

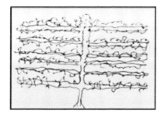

Or this:

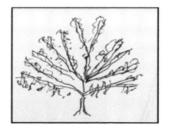

Or even this:

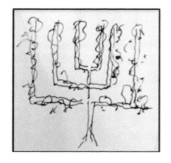

And then you have to get your head round the instructions. I've taken the following instructions from the venerable Royal Horticultural Society, and if the RHS says to do it a certain way, you do it that way. It does assume a certain amount of understanding about different parts of a tree: what you need to know is that the 'maiden stem' is the main stem, and that the first,

second, third buds, and so on, are exactly that. And then you're
flying (albeit quite slowly).

The first thing is to get a tree. You can espalier pears, apples,
figs, peaches, nectarines – pretty much any fruit tree, I think. As
well as looking beautiful and very grown-up, fruit trees trained
this way create incredibly good conditions for the fruit itself
because, if you think about it, the air can get at it. Picking the fruit
is easier too.

This is a recipe for a simple espaliered shape:

1. Get yourself an unfeathered maiden (don't ask – just request this
   when you're buying), and then cut the main stem down to about
   30cm from the ground. It feels quite brutal doing this, but it's
   intrinsic to success later on. (As an aside, it's the same with a lot
   of clematis, which really should be chopped down to a certain
   height when they first go in the ground – but that is a whole
   other story.)

2. Identify the top three buds (before you start panicking, remember to consult handy diagram) and let them grow out during
   spring. Then fix some horizontal wires on the wall, and get
   some canes, too, for good measure. Train the top one up a
   vertical cane, and tie the others to canes set at 45 degrees to the
   main stem. In November, bend these VERY carefully until they
   are horizontal and tie them to the horizontal wires that you put
   in at the beginning of the process. Basically, in spring you're

merely suggesting to the new branches that they should be going in a particular direction; new branches are very flexible and obedient and will go wherever you want them to go, but they can't take instructions quickly and will snap if bent before they've done their spring warm-up. By November, these limbs have got their minds around where they're heading, and just need a little nudge. A bit like yoga, really.

Now look at the two horizontal branches, all neat and tidy and straight, and you'll see that there's still the main stem going up in between. Cut this back to 45cm from where the two lower arms branch out, leaving three buds again: two buds to form the next horizontal layer and the top bud to form the new leader (vertical stem).

The following year, train the second tier in the same way as the first. Cut back any bits growing out of the leader, as these will sap energy from the stems you're concentrating on. Cut any side shoots from the horizontal arms back to three leaves above the bunch of leaves denoting the start of the current season's growth. I understand that this is the bit that may make your head explode, so I suggest you refer to a diagram again here.

Repeat the process until the tree has produced its final tier and grown horizontally to fill its allotted space. Then allow two shoots to grow: tie them to the top wire and cut them back to within 2.5cm (1in) of their base the following winter.

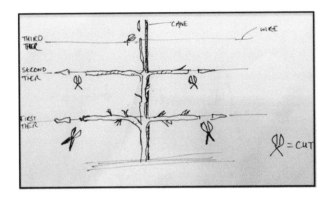

It's incredibly important to remove all blossom in the first three years – it'll seem like infanticide and, also slightly mad, to remove pretty flowers, but doing this makes sure that the tree puts all its energies into growing and doesn't get distracted by trying to produce fruit, which requires a huge amount of energy.

I'm longing for you to give this a go. I haven't got any spare vertical spaces, and you've got some gorgeous walls which would look fantastic with an elegant espalier or two. Please? I'll help.

Gardener

Dear Gardener,

Wow – thank you so much for that. You really have explained it well. I am inspired now to put in two or three on the right side of the garden – they will look fab. I may make a pear tarte tatin today to celebrate. I can caramelise the pears now (I've got three in my fruit bowl), then nip out and get some ready-made puff pastry, and *voilà* – a very delicious autumn pudding. The next recipe is one of my faves. It is probably the one I get most compliments for and which quite a few of my friends really like making. It's great for entertaining because you can make it ahead. It's made with the 'instapastry' and is not at all hard, just do it step-by-step. You can also put the juice of half a lemon in the frangipane if you like lemon – it's up to you.

Pear and almond tart

SERVES 6

For the pastry
110g (4oz) butter, hard from the fridge
175g (6oz) plain flour
1 tbsp icing sugar
½ tsp vanilla essence

For the filling
150g (5oz) blanched or ground almonds
150g (5oz) butter, softened
150g (5oz) caster sugar
1 egg plus one egg yolk
45g (1½ oz) plain flour

450g (16 oz) tinned pear halves

Preheat the oven to 180°C. To make the pastry case for the tart, put all the ingredients into a food processor and whizz until you get breadcrumb lookalikes. Press the mixture with your hands, like Plasticine, into a 22cm (9 inch) square flan tin. Put in the fridge for an hour,or if short of time, in the freezer for 20 minutes. Bake in the oven until light brown then leave it to cool. It is then ready to fill.

Now make the almond paste (or frangipane). If you are using blanched almonds, put them in a food processor and grind to a fine crumb. If you are using ground almond, no need – obviously!

Beat the butter until softened then beat in the sugar. Now gradually beat in the whole egg and egg yolk. Stir in the almonds and flour. Put your delicious mix into your cooled pastry case. Open your tin of pears, drain off the liquid, then press the pear halves into the mixture with a gap between each one – place a final trimmed pear in the centre.

Heat your oven to 180°C again and put your tart in the oven for about 40–50 minutes. When you take it out, the almond paste will have risen slightly and will be almost covering the pears, and should be a golden brown. Leave to cool or serve slightly warm with cream, ice cream or crème fraîche.

Cook

7

Dahlias and aubergines

Dear Gardener,

I have been developing a bit of a thing about dahlias in the last couple of years. They have always been known as a bit of a bonkers flower. Everyone seems to have a story about an old aunt who grew dahlias. My sister said the French woman my parents bought their house from grew dahlias everywhere. My in-laws announced the other day that they have dug up their dahlias as they are just too much hassle to grow. Do you think this is true? Is there an easy way to grow dahlias? Even if there isn't, don't you think the mad riot of colour they produce throughout early autumn is worth it? Dahlias to me are like a final salute to summer, surrounding the autumn table with a last laugh.

Cook

Dear Cook

Nothing is ever too much hassle to at least try to grow. Dahlias really were considered infra dig (sorry) until a few years ago, when people realised that they fitted in so neatly with whole vintage

DAHLIAS

thing, giving colour and blowsiness in spades (I can't stop it, sorry) after the peonies and roses had gone. I was at a client's yesterday admiring the dahlias that are still giving it their best in mid-November. A few pounds' worth of tubers had filled a border, as well as vases in the house. I'm a gardener who likes to find the easy route: you can go to the bother of lifting dahlias, but frankly, I like to leave them in the ground and just see. You live in a fairly warm area, so at least a few of them should be OK. My mother leaves all hers in, and the shoots come up year after year – she is in Dorset, though; I shouldn't like to speak for anyone in Scotland.

And the colours – I agree with you. Purples, oranges, pinks: all the colours that really shouldn't go with each other, yet they do. They sit as well together as a group of semi-precious stones. (I'm just dreaming of a bracelet of amethyst, rose quartz and citrine.)

My current dahlia chart-toppers are 'Cabana Banana', 'Ambition', 'Otto's Thrill', 'Wine-Eyed Jill', 'Tahoma Moonshot', 'Dark Spirit' and 'Café au Lait'. You could go for a tasteful colour combo, or simply throw them all in together. Somewhat haphazard, I know, but somehow this randomness sits fantastically well in the border at a time of year when any colour is a bonus – one feels positively endowed with good cheer as their crazy shapes pop up among the browning leaves surrounding them. And anyway, how could you NOT buy a dahlia called 'Cabana Banana'?

The news from here is: I HAVE FINALLY MADE A TOMATO SAUCE THAT BOTH THE CHILDREN WILL EAT. As the daughter of an Italian, I really should have got the hang of this years ago, but I think I've been going wrong by overthinking it. Passata, olive oil, garlic and basil in the pan for twenty minutes, and success in a pasta bowl. Do you remember when we used to weep in despair at those cookery books which were basically 'What children should eat but in reality are unlikely to go within twenty paces of' recipes?

So here I am, patting myself on the back at having provided something delicious but pretty basic. Have you any basic dishes all'Italiana that you think might go down well here? Smuggling in a vegetable or two is your challenge...

Till the soil till next time,

Gardener

Dear Gardener,

My mother used to make Parmigiana in the 1980s, when no one else did (she learned to cook in Perugia for a year when she was eighteen), and I immediately loved it then, just as I do now. I know it is in a lot of restaurants but I think it's a great supper with a chicken breast and a green salad.

I was sent to Italy every summer as a teenager with some Italian friends of hers. They owned (and still own) a restaurant in Rome called the Babington Tearooms. Their uncle owned a nightclub in Porto Santo Stefano called Strega del Mare (translates to 'Witch of the Sea'). Apparently it was quite a hotspot and a favourite of the glitterati of those days. My memories of tea rooms, nightclubs and hot summers spent on the Tuscan coast are a constant source of inspiration for me and remind me how much I absolutely love Italy and making Italian food. Quite simply, it tastes so good.

Parmigiana

SERVES 8

7 aubergines

1–2 tablespoons olive oil (if baking)

3–4 tablespoons olive oil (if frying)

Home-made tomato sauce (see below – or bought, in a jar, if you are in a hurry)

200g (7oz) Parmesan cheese shavings

2 balls mozzarella, cut into bite-size pieces

150g (5oz) of cheddar cheese, grated

For the tomato sauce

Olive oil

2 red onions, chopped

1 garlic clove

2 x 400g (14oz) tins chopped tomatoes

½ tsp sugar

Salt and pepper

This home-made tomato sauce is really easy, so the jar option can easily be avoided. Soften two onions in the oil over a medium heat then add the clove of garlic, tomatoes and sugar, and season with the salt and pepper. Cook over a low heat for 20 minutes, then liquidise until smooth.

Preheat the oven to 160°C. Cut your aubergines into circles about half an inch thick. Fry them in the olive oil until golden brown. If you want to use less oil, brown them in the oven with a little oil. Now it's time for layering. In a square-shaped dish put a layer of aubergines followed by a layer of tomato sauce, a little pepper and a layer of cheddar, spot a few bits of mozzarella around and then sprinkle over the shaved Parmesan. Repeat until you have used up everything and finished with a sprinkling of Parmesan on the top. Cook in the oven for about 45 minutes.

Cook

Dear Cook

Sounds mouthwatering: I always thought that Parmigiana was too tricky to attempt, but I think I'll be brave enough to have a go. A question: don't you have to do the weird salting thing to the aubergines? That's the faffing-about bit that has always put me off in the past.

Gardener

Dear Gardener

Apparently, these days all aubergines have been cultivated in a way that makes the salting unnecessary. I don't bother any more.

Cook

8

Instagardens and Instasupper

Dear Gardener,

I am wondering about 'instant' gardens. Whenever I watch home-improvement shows, where gardens with old plastic toys are turned into showstopper small gardens packed with plants and style, I shed a tear (to be honest I cry, properly). These tears are shed for a number of reasons; some for the insanely happy recipients on the show, some for my own chaos that resides outside, and some for the regret for my own lazy (some might say downright slovenly) habits which means that nothing ever gets done apart from the bare necessities. Is there such a thing as an Instagarden? I know I could put in loads of bedding plants such as geraniums, but what else could lift the place? Is the result only 'instant', like a new top that loses its allure two days later owing to the fact that one really needs a whole new outfit, or do you think it would or could create a lasting happiness? So, let's have it, Gardener: 'The Shortcut'.

Cook

Dear Cook,

This, I promise, is as easy as pie…

An Instagarden you desire, so an Instagarden I shall deliver. The trick is to keep it simple. So, for a small patch:

Take one rose that will repeat (in a non-digestive way):

1 x Rosa 'Mary Rose'
At her feet, put catmint…

3 x Nepeta 'Walker's Low'
    and

3 x Geranium 'Rozanne'
For colour from May to September.

You need a bit of an acid-green zing now, to stop the mauves being too wishy-washy:

3 x Alchemilla mollis
Lady's mantle will appear everywhere in your garden once you introduce it – but who's complaining at a free plant?

Pop in the bulbs at the aforementioned appropriate time:

5 x Tulipa 'Purissima'
    and

7 x Tulipa 'Queen of Night'

And we need a little more late-summer interest:

3 x Verbena bonariensis

and

3 x Gaura lindheimeri

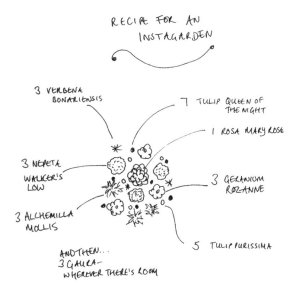

Apart from the rose, which you need to deadhead in order to keep the blooms coming, you need do little else apart from chop things back when they look untidy.

Bob's your uncle and Fanny is, possibly, your aunt: Instagarden – which will look good next year too.

Your turn now: Instasupper please.

Gardener

Dear Gardener

Instasuppers fill me with delight. They are quick but still delicious. I am constantly told what a good 'baker' I am but this is simply not true; my best Instafood is Instapastry – I use it for all tarts. I use it for pear and almond tart, I use it for lemon tart, and for a savoury version I put Parmesan in it and use it for a fabulous goat's cheese and red onion tart – I think I have literally changed lives with this pastry. I did a cooking day at my house a few years ago and this recipe was so well received by the participants, and I noticed over the coming months that many of them started making their own tarts. I attribute this entirely to Instapastry, the recipe for which I first came across in a Claire Macdonald recipe. I am not entirely sure I could make a shortcrust pastry now: it's been so long since I tried, and frankly I get many more compliments for its sly cousin, Instapastry.

A popular Instasupper in my house is cod (or any white firm fish) with tomato and butterbean sauce. This can take as little as 10 minutes, especially if you are using a bought bottle of tomato sauce.

Cod with tomato and butterbean sauce

SERVES 4

1 tub of shop-bought tomato sauce or home-made tomato sauce
250g (9oz) tin butterbeans, drained
4 cod fillets
1 packet of Parma ham (optional)
Serve with ripped-up basil leaves

Heat the tomato sauce in a pan and add the butterbeans. Meanwhile cook your fish in the oven, and if you've got some Parma ham, put that in the oven, too, to crisp up.

Fill a large bowl with the tomato and butterbeans. Put the cooked fish on top and crown it with some crispy Parma ham. Rip up some basil leaves on top.

You can use the tomato and butterbean sauce with sausages too, and you can swap the butterbeans for a tin of brown lentils. Add some fresh thyme to the sauce and melt in some feta cheese when you add your cooked sausages. Very hearty but very delicious.

Instapastry

(A SHORTCUT SHORTCRUST A BIT LIKE SHORTBREAD)

110g (4oz) butter, hard from the fridge
175g (6oz) plain flour
1 tbsp icing sugar
½ tsp vanilla essence

Preheat the oven to 180°C. For this instant marvel, put all the ingredients into a food processor and whizz until you get breadcrumb lookalikes. Then simply press the mixture with your hands into a 22cm (9 inch) flan tin like Plasticine. Put in the fridge for an hour, or if short of time, in the freezer for 20 minutes. Bake in the oven until light brown. The pastry will shrink from the sides a bit but you can always press it back in place with a teaspoon. Leave it to cool; it is then ready to fill. I am inclined to say 'Magic' at this point. I sometimes make one-and-a-half quantities of above recipe just to make sure I have enough, or double the amount if you are a using a larger tin.

Cook

INSTAPASTRY

½ TEASPOON
VANILLA ESSENCE

175g PLAIN FLOUR

1 TBLSPOON ICING SUGAR

110g
BUTTER

INGREDIENTS

1. WHIZZ ALL INGREDIENTS
   IN FOOD PROCESSOR

2. PRESS MIXTURE
   INTO FLAN TIN

3. BAKE IN A 180 C
   OVEN UNTIL LIGHT
   BROWN

4. LEAVE TO COOL

9

Lemon trees and lemon tart

Dear Gardener,

As I lie like a large leg of lamb roasting in the sun in Corfu, I am looking around at the produce on offer. Huge lemons hanging off trees like overweight Christmas decorations, olive trees magnificent in their Mediterranean setting, an almond tree with velvet purses attached to its branches and the promise of delicious nuts in a month or so. And finally the figs, still green but already giving off their sweet aroma. I'm thinking of almond tarts, juicy figs baking with Greek honey, tapenade on crusty bread and sharp lemon juice on fresh tuna with a feta and mango salad. I think I must be hungry. Anyway, my question to you is about growing these Mediterranean gems on our chilly shores. Without a conservatory, can a fig tree or lemon tree survive? The other day, at Chelsea Flower Show, my friend insisted on buying a kumquat tree and a lemon tree. Was this rash and foolhardy or brave and optimistic? Will an olive tree make it through an English January? I'm not even sure I've ever seen an almond (currently my favourite nut) tree *en Angleterre*? Thoughts on citrus fruit?

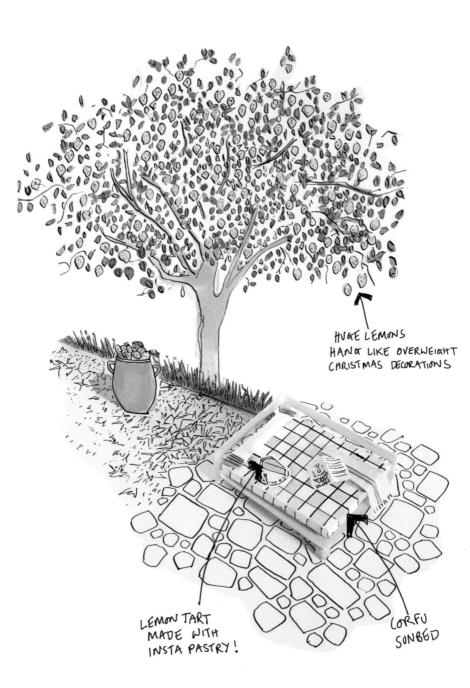

HUGE LEMONS
HANG LIKE OVERWEIGHT
CHRISTMAS DECORATIONS

LEMON TART
MADE WITH
INSTA PASTRY!

CORFU
SUNBED

Back to the tuna steaks with a feta and mango salad. This is a great summer supper and probably my signature dish. It is all about the salad, although the tuna is obviously the main event.

Marinate the tuna in olive oil and lots of lime juice – by this I mean squeeze the limes and leave them in among the tuna steaks while they are marinating.

The salad is made with feta cut into chunks, mango chopped into small squares, spring onions neatly chopped and a couple of oranges peeled and cut into segments with the pith removed. Add your watercress (I like watercress as it is peppery, but you could use other small salad leaves if you prefer). Combine all the ingredients and add a lime and olive oil dressing (recipe in my Salad Top Ten on p. 28).

Then cook the tuna (it will have partly 'cooked' in the lime juice). I like doing it on a grillade so it has the criss-crosses, but by all means do it on the BBQ – but golden rule (I know you know): do not overcook it.

Serve with small roasted new potatoes with a little rosemary stirred through while cooking.

Must go: I am starving and literally salivating.

Cook

Dear Cook

I didn't know I knew but I know now – though there's a fine line, I feel, between tuna cooked just right and tuna undercooked to the extent that the fishiness takes over. Horses for courses. (Or fishes for dishes?)

On the fruit tree issue, my initial reaction is 'kumquats – really?' I do find it totally bizarre that you're basically eating a mini-orange, skin and all. Having said that, I was to an extent converted by the Corfu salad of local smoked ham and preserved kumquats – I'm not normally one for candied peel but that combination was rather wonderful, though I'm wondering whether the flavours were somewhat enhanced by the water's-edge setting and the endless local rosé.

If you're going to go down the road of lemon trees (I would like to find an actual road of lemon trees) then what you need is a conservatory or orangery (lemonery?). Lemons just can't take the cold. Kumquats can take a bit more than other citrus, but you do need to bring them on. Plant-health alert on central heating: this makes it too hot for them. High maintenance, or what?

Which reminds me, thank you for that easy one-pot pastry recipe. Did you also use it for the lemon tart we had the other evening? It was fabulous and even better than the one I used to buy and pass off as my own from the Roux brothers' deli by Pimlico Green. I used to love that little patch of perfection in an area that I believe now likes to consider itself part of Belgravia. I'd walk up from the tiniest flat in Cambridge Street; crossing the great divider of Ebury Bridge was like coming out of the other side of the wardrobe into Narnia. There lay Pimlico still, sort of – but smarter in every sense. The delis, the galleries and La Poule au Pot, which was the best restaurant for romantic meals. I always tried to engineer a date there with whichever boyfriend was the most obliging at the time.

(I won't ask for a lamb recipe. Sizzle sizzle…)

Gardener

Dear Gardener

My lemon tart is, of course, made with Instapastry. NB you can make the pastry and freeze it but I find that it really is best eaten on the day of baking if at all possible.

Lemon tart

SERVES 6

Instapastry

110g (4oz) butter, hard from the fridge

175g (6oz) plain flour

1 tbsp icing sugar

½ tsp vanilla essence

Filling

4 eggs

1 egg yolk (optional)

170g (6oz) caster sugar

150ml (5fl oz) double cream

Zest and juice of 2 lemons
Icing sugar, for dusting

Preheat the oven to 180°C. Put all the instapastry ingredients into a food processor and whizz until you get breadcrumb lookalikes. Then simply press the mixture with your hands into a 22cm (9 inch) flan tin like Plasticine. Put in the fridge for an hour, or if short of time, in the freezer for 20 minutes. Blind bake (no need for baking beans) for 20–25 minutes. Leave to cool.

Meanwhile make your filling. Mix the eggs and extra egg yolk, if using, with the sugar. Stir in the cream then add the lemon zest and juice. I do this in a food processor. I love lemons so I tend to put in a bit more juice – maybe a third lemon, juice and zest, as I like it really sharp. I think you just have to taste it as you go along, with a clean teaspoon.

Pour the mixture into the cooled pastry case: I do this on an oven tray as sometimes there are cracks in my pastry and it seeps out. Also, I don't like walking gingerly to the oven hoping the mixture won't spill over the top. Just do the case-filling as near to the oven as you can! Bake for 50 minutes until almost set. Remove the tart from the oven and take it out of the tin. When cool, dust with icing sugar.

I made this again yesterday and suddenly had the desire to 'tart up the tart'. I got a packet of flaked almonds from the cupboard, put them into a frying pan that I'd already heated up, added some honey and it turned into a delicious topping. I put this all over the top of my tart and put blackberries in the gaps. I must admit, it looked and tasted great.

Cook

10

Rhubarb rhubarb

Dear Gardener,

My dad always used to say 'Rhubarb rhubarb', probably to keep himself as sane as possible in the midst of five children constantly asking him insane repetitive questions. So 'Rhubarb rhubarb' means… well, anything, really; it is just about wittering on about absolute rubbish. It is also rather a comforting slogan, giving one time to pause for thought when words fail. On a more philosophical slant, it really means that everything is a complete load of twaddle.

More importantly, I just love rhubarb. I love the word, I love the pink colour, I love the smell and I adore the taste. Could you give me some info on growing rhubarb? Does one buy a 'crown' (I love this idea, too – maybe rhubarb should be given royal status) and put it anywhere in the ground? What are its ideal growing conditions? Would it grow well in a city garden?

Must go and make a something with rhubarb. I recently served a very good rhubarb yoghurt. It was really simple and so delicious.

Rhubarb yoghurt

SERVES 4

400g (14oz) rhubarb
1 tbsp sugar, or to taste
350g (12oz) very good-quality Greek yoghurt
125g (4½ oz) pomegranate seeds
Mint leaves, roughly chopped

For the nut brittle
Approx. 70g (2½ oz) granulated sugar
100g (3½ oz) nuts such as pecans or almonds

Make a rhubarb compote by simmering the rhubarb in a pan with a little water and the sugar, to taste. Cool down the compote, then put a thick layer of it at the bottom of a glass. Next add enough Greek yoghurt that the glass is three-quarters full. Now stir in the pomegranate seeds and roughly chopped mint.

Here's the tricky bit – making the brittle. Heat the oven to 180°C and roast the nuts for about 7 minutes – keep checking them so they don't burn. Now cover the bottom of a heavy-based pan with half a centimetre of granulated sugar. Do not stir it. Wait until it caramelises, then tip the nuts into it. Pour the whole mixture onto a sheet of greaseproof paper.

If you are tired and this sounds overwhelming just sprinkle some nuts onto the top of your yoghurt. Happy eating, and have a right royal day!

Cook

Dear Cook

I have a confession to make: I have never grown rhubarb until this year, as I've always been a bit put off by forcing etc – it all looked rather complicated. However, I didn't mess it up, which means it's foolproof and I'm confident that you'll be able to manage it (that really looks as if there's a dig there, but I promise you it's unintended – just heartfelt, hahahaha).

Here's the plan:

1. Choose where you're going to grow the rhubarb (obviously).

2. Get rid of weeds (obviously).

3. Add manure (composted and of the equine variety. Remove any deposits of the canine variety).

4. Buy 2 or 3 crowns (or pot-grown rhubarb). You won't need much more as they need to be planted about a metre apart.

The forcing bit isn't that complicated, and you don't actually have to do it unless you want your crop to come a few weeks earlier. You cover the crown with one of those forcing jars or just even an upturned pot – you're aiming to block out all the light, so cover any holes in the pot. When the stems reach the top – which they will do, as they are desperate for light – they are ready for harvesting.

I'm off to compote.

Gardener

11

Novel suppers

Dear Cook

Heeeeeeeeeeellllllppppppppppp!!!!!!!

Just looked in the diary (helllppp again!) and I see it's my turn to make lunch for my book club tomorrow – TOMORROW! And I've done nothing for it. Absolute zero. I blame it on the electronic diary; it constantly surprises me by springing today's events upon me without warning, and even if it attempts to tell me the day before, I don't notice as the alerts never come when you're sitting down with a cup of tea with the virtual diary page open; they come when I'm driving or in a hole in the ground with big fat gardening gloves on. So they get ignored. I fear it is back to the good old, actual, real diary for me, much to the horror of everyone in the office who needs to know my constant whereabouts. What's wrong with speaking words and just asking where I am, I ask?

In a nutshell, I'm going to get back at 12:30 tomorrow. What on earth can I proffer which will look as if I care? Because I do care, I really do.

If it helps, I've a butternut squash here that is begging to be eaten. As I grew it, I feel it's only right that it gets used for its proper purpose rather than being glazed and placed artistically at the centre of a seasonal display. An autumnal glazed gourd installation is a second option, I suppose...

Gardener

Dear Gardener

Here's a really delicious 30-minute soup and the reason it's so good is the tomato backdrop. It adds a richness and depth of flavour you simply don't get with butternut squash on its own. The spices give it a fabulous warmth that, though I say it myself, is unbeatable. My top tip for the future is that you can buy frozen butternut squash, which cuts time and hassle and fear of large, knobbly vegetables. This soup is quick, and on a cold, dank November day it really is just the ticket.

Spicy and warm tomato and butternut squash soup

SERVES 8

2 red onions, finely chopped
Butter, for frying
1 butternut squash, peeled and cut into pieces, or 2 bags of frozen
   butternut squash
½ tsp chilli powder
½ tsp paprika
½ tsp ground ginger
Salt and pepper
2 x 400g (14oz) tins chopped tomatoes
500ml (1 pint) stock
A dash of lemon juice, or to taste
Milk, cream or 200ml (7fl oz) coconut milk (optional)

Sweat the onion in butter until tender. Add your butternut squash, cooking until it has softened a little. Add your dry spices and some salt and pepper. This should take about 5–10 minutes overall. Once everything looks soft enough, add your tomatoes, stock and lemon juice. Leave to simmer for another 10–15 minutes. Liquidise and add more salt or pepper, to taste. If you want, you can add a bit of milk or cream, or even half a tin of coconut milk.

Follow up with a smoked salmon pâté, which you can make while the soup is cooking.

Smoked salmon pâté

I have to admit this is not really a pâté – there is no gelatine or anything involved and it takes only about 2 minutes. However, everyone seems to 'oooh' and 'ahhh' over it and ask me 'Did you make this? It's delicious', to which I smugly reply: YES.

175g (6oz) of smoked salmon scraps
75g (2½ oz) unsalted butter
Juice of one lemon
60ml (2fl oz) single cream
A handful of dill (delicious but optional)
Pepper
Cucumber slices and dill, to garnish

Cut up your salmon and put in the food processor. Gently melt your butter then add it to the salmon along with the lemon juice, cream and dill (if using). Blend until smooth and season with pepper but no salt. Put into individual ramekins, cover with cling film and put in the fridge for a couple of hours. Decorate with slices of cucumber and a sprig of dill and serve with hot buttered brown toast. The pâté is also suitable for freezing.

Sardine pâté

This is a delicious pâté that I had in a restaurant in the Alps. I've made a very simple version of it – it's a humble offering but rather nice on a bit of sourdough for lunch with a rocket salad on the side.

2 tins of sardines
100g (3½ oz) low-fat cream cheese
A dollop or two of crème fraîche
Salt and lots of pepper
Juice of half a lemon

Whizz everything together in a mini food processor, finishing off with salt and pepper and the lemon juice. It's not the greatest colour, I have to admit, which is why you need a rocket salad with it.

I always think of sardines as a bit of a superfood so this pâté always makes me feel healthy, which adds to the general feeling of well-being while tucking into this simple fare.

For more substantial food for the book club you could make a fish pie, and if you are in a hurry you could use the frozen fish pie mix you can get from supermarkets, make a vermouth-type white sauce and put a bit of puff pastry on the top.

Here's a really good seafood salad recipe, too:

Seafood salad

SERVES 8

8 prepared squid tubes, cut into pieces
8 scallops
8 peeled raw tiger prawns
2 tbsp olive oil
Salt and pepper
1 large red or orange pepper chopped into slices
8 spring onions, finely sliced
10 olives, halved
4 tbsp Greek yoghurt
4 tbsp capers, roughly chopped
Chopped dill and parsley
Juice of 1 lime, or to taste

Toss the squid, scallops and prawns in the olive oil and season with salt and pepper. Pan-fry the prawns for 3 minutes and remove to a large salad bowl. Now add the squid to the pan, fry for 30–60 seconds and add to the prawns. Finally, sear the scallops on each side and pan-fry for no more than a minute, then add to the squid and prawns.

Add all the other ingredients to the bowl, mix everything together and season well, adding lime juice to taste. Serve with French bread.

NB If you are scared of squid (I totally understand) you could do this just with prawns – it would still be yummy.

Goat's cheese, red onion and red pepper tart

This is not a quick recipe like the others I've suggested, but it is one of my favourite things to eat for lunch. You would have to remember you had people coming so that you could make it the day before or, if you had time, during the morning. Once again I use the Instapastry recipe, but with Parmesan this time.

SERVES 6

For the pastry
175g (6oz) flour
110g (4oz) butter
50g (1½ oz) Parmesan cheese, finely grated
1 tbsp of chopped thyme (optional)

For the onion jam
25g (1oz) butter
25g (1oz) soft brown sugar
1 tbsp balsamic vinegar
2 red onions, finely sliced
Salt and pepper

For the filling
2 red peppers
3 eggs
300ml (10½ fl oz) double cream
175g (6oz) soft goat's cheese
A pinch of nutmeg
Salt and pepper (ground white pepper works well here)

Preheat the oven to 180°C. To make the pastry, whizz together the ingredients (including the thyme, if using) in a food processor until it looks like breadcrumbs. Press the mix into a flan tin with your fingers, cover with cling film and put it in the fridge for an hour. (If you are in a hurry, put it in the freezer for 20 minutes.) Bake in the oven until the pastry is light brown in colour. Let it cool.

Turn up the oven to 200°C and roast your peppers for 20 minutes. Let them cool, then cut into strips. (You can easily use peppers from a jar to save time.)

Now for the red onion jam: melt the butter and add the sugar, vinegar and onions. Cook on a low heat for 20 minutes or until the onions are very soft. You could even add a slug of red wine to the mixture during the cooking, and a bit of water to thin it out if it gets very thick. Put to one side.

For the flan filling, set the oven to 150°C. Combine the eggs and cream in a bowl with a fork, then pass the mixture through a sieve into another bowl. Add the goat's cheese, nutmeg, salt and pepper.

Spread the onion jam over the bottom of the tart case, then pour in the egg mix and finally dot the red peppers over the top in an artistic fashion. Bake the flan for 40–50 minutes. You want the custard to have set but have a slight wobble to it.

Serve for lunch, with a salad.

Cook

12

Roses and summer feasts

Dear Cook,

The climbing rose outside your back door is exquisite. I have never seen it before and had no idea what it was, but thanks to helpful social media followers I've identified it as Rosa 'Desprez à Fleurs Jaunes'. I used to loathe yellowish flowers, and yellowish roses in particular, but maybe it's a sign of 'maturity' that these gorgeous shades of primrose, lemon and apricot can now stop me in my tracks. 'Ghislaine de Féligonde' and 'Alister Stella Gray' are equally fabulous. Perhaps it's the way that these shades go so perfectly with old brick walls (I'm not sure how successful they would be against a stark white background, where the deeper pink of 'Zéphirine Drouhin' looks so good).

I'm working on a list for your twin borders: I think trouble-free and as much bang for your buck is the way to go here. 'Gertrude Jekyll' (how is it that when people talk about roses, they seem to be referring to old friends?), 'Eglantyne' and 'The Generous Gardener' will all tone well alongside each other; I'd plant them in threes – so three plants of 'Eglantyne', in a triangle, with the plants about two feet apart from each other. And so on. You can cut the flowers but they'll probably only last a day or two inside,

which is therefore a reason to have as many of the plants as possible outside. Rose gardens have become somewhat unfashionable, partly due to disease and partly due to the look of so many bare sticks poking out of the soil when the plants are not in flower, but that's no reason not to have roses in the border. Stand up against fashion and see what happens! Look at the dahlia!

Scent is one of the big pluses of the rose (you can't beat the fragrance of 'Ispahan'). And as an added bonus, roses that smell fabulous are indeed fabulous for cooking. This I know for a fact; what I don't know is what you'd actually put them in. Do you ever actually use them? Or are roses that one ingredient you

realise you don't have when you get to the bottom of the recipe, and just leave out? Are they something I can throw into a summer salad? Actually, the thought makes me feel a little queasy: I'm not a big fan of edible flowers in bowls of leaves. I've tried to create a 'Summer Feast' straight from the glossy pages of the Sunday supplements; I was seduced, I think, by a photo of exquisite-looking salads adorned with a sprinkle of pansy petals. But on eating – well, the petals tasted like petals in a vegetation kind of way. I do need a good summer salad up my sleeve – not literally. Any ideas?

Gardener

Dear Gardener,

A really excellent crowd-pleaser that my teacher at Leiths, Sue Spaull, gave me years ago is a Thai green chicken salad. It is absolutely brilliant, and I meanly have not passed it on to anyone since then. But, as you've asked, here it is:

Thai green chicken salad

SERVES 6

4–5 chicken breasts, skin off

For the curry paste
4 green chillies
3 spring onions, roughly chopped
3 garlic cloves
A handful of coriander, including the stalks
2.5cm (1 inch) fresh ginger, peeled and chopped
Zest of 1 lemon
1 tsp shrimp paste
1 tsp vegetable oil
1 tsp jalapeño sauce
1 tbsp black peppercorns
1 tsp ground cumin
1 tsp ground coriander
1 tsp ground lemongrass powder or 1 crushed lemongrass
1 tsp salt

For the sauce
400g (14oz) tin coconut milk
150ml (5fl oz) Greek yoghurt
120ml (4fl oz) mayonnaise
2 tbsp mango chutney
Salt and pepper
Lime juice (as much as you like the taste of)

Preheat the oven to 180° then roast the chicken breasts for about 25 minutes or until cooked through. Cool, then chop into bite-size chunks.

Blend all the ingredients for the curry paste in a food processor until smooth. If you haven't got all the ingredients (e.g. if you can't find lemongrass powder) don't panic; it will still be nice – also you could, if in a hurry, use 2 heaped tablespoons of bought paste and then it becomes another Instameal, though it is much more delicious if you use your own.

Fry 3 tablespoons of the curry paste in a dry frying pan over a medium heat until it looks a bit curdled. This will take about 3 minutes. (The remaining paste can be stored in a covered jar in the fridge for up to one week.) Add the coconut milk to the pan, cook for 2 minutes then remove from the heat and leave to cool completely.

Stir your yoghurt, mayonnaise and chutney into the coconut mixture, season with the salt and pepper, then pour over the chicken. Add lime juice to taste, and loads of coriander.

Please try this next time you have a crowd – they will love it. Serve with couscous with a bit of broccoli and herbs tossed in, or with rice. It's a winner.

Cook

Dear Cook,

OMG you're right – it was absolutely perfect. Delicious. A triumph. I must admit, when I first saw the recipe, I thought, 'I'll just nip to the supermarket and get me a jar of curry paste', but I'd have had to confess and then you'd never let me hear the end of it, in a non-verbal but disappointed-face kind of way. So with a sigh I hit the shelves, which took some time because, although most items are located pretty obviously, I'll have you know that locating shrimp paste is not at all intuitive.

The good news is the salad went down a storm (have I

exhausted all clichés yet? I could go on). It's got a sort of zingy freshness and – surprise, surprise – doesn't have that slightly metallic tang that seems to be obligatory with all jar sauces. Although a big part of me rails at the fact that cooking good food should make one feel as if one has achieved something, the simple truth is that it did. I must just remember that providing good food three times a day is not an achievement, it's enslavement.

I even put flowers on the table – just a bunch of dahlias grabbed from the farm shop as I forgot to cut mine back and they've stopped flowering. I'm making lists and lists of dahlias for clients' gardens, and rather controversially I'm sneaking in a few gladioli. I'd like to say I'm at the forefront of their renaissance in terms of what's hot and what's not, but I remember them featuring significantly at a party of yours aeons ago?

Gardener

13

Entertaining with gladness and gladioli

Dear Gardener,

I think I would be glad to grow gladioli. I have liked them for nigh on a decade and indeed I had great big vases of them at my fortieth birthday – I'm delighted you remembered. They looked great, and as they come in so many colours they really went with my decoration. I had white tablecloths on round tables with different-coloured linen napkins and mixed bunches of gladioli in the centre of each table. There were menus on each table with a picture of a woman and a dog, captioned 'In dog years you're dead'. A friend of my husband's commented on my black sense of humour; I thought it was highly amusing myself.

I arranged an Italian feast for my guests and I can remember the menu: deep-fried courgette flowers, arancini and melon and figs to begin with, followed by a trio of home-made pasta dishes. One was with a fresh tomato sauce (still one of my favourites), one with *vongole*, and ravioli with ricotta and lemon.

Next, we had saltimbocca (but with chicken because I don't like

eating veal) with tiny roast potatoes, roasted tomatoes and roasted
courgette ribbons with a rocket salad. To finish we had peach
sorbet and roasted peaches.

The whole thing was cooked by an Italian chef who insisted
that she could cook for sixty on a two-oven aga. As a result, the
fire brigade came three times (all ladies present were quite
pleased) and lunch could definitely be described as a long one.

I even served macaroons at the end with cups of delicious
espresso (this was before macaroons were popular) and their
colours looked so pretty with all the different linens and gladioli.
It was a great day, and to remind me of it I really would like to
plant some of those Dame Edna specimens. But I'm afraid
macaroons have nearly reached cupcake status in my book, which
means they go into my Room 101.

Are there any trade secrets before I arrive at my next 'significant
birthday' – 'significant birthday' being probably one of the worst
expressions of recent times... Almost as bad as 'significant other'?

Yours insignificantly

Cook

Dear Cook

I'm fairly cringing – 'significant other' is bad, but my worst phrase
has to be 'hubby', and also when people refer to their tiny baby
son as 'little man'. The former just because it's awful in the way
that 'holibobs' and 'famalam' are awful; the latter – well, I don't
really know. Maybe it's because it seems to be putting a huge
amount of pressure on a three-month-old. And you can bet your
bottom dollar that anyone calling their baby daughter 'little lady'
would get into dreadful trouble.

That lunch was so funny – I'm sure the chef was on the cooking wine. It was, though, truly a day to remember, as the food was (eventually) delicious, and the firefighters were an added bonus. It all looked fabulous too: out in the garden with perfect weather. I was amazed how many tables you fitted into the space.

What I really admire about you is that you just don't panic. Supper for six? There you go. Lunch for sixty? No problem. What do you do first when decide on yet another thing that involves people coming into your house, sitting at your table and eating your food? Do you make loads of lists? And are flowers always on that list?

The gladioli were stunning – my current favourite is Gladiolus 'Black Jack', which I grow lots and lots of, in neat rows between the salads in the veg beds. Glads don't take up much ground space at all, so I order them along with the dahlias, then simply pop them in the soil a few centimetres away from each other, which makes for easy weeding as well, letting me recognise what's growing where. They are so easy – just remember to stake them. Every year, I say I'm going to stake them, then I always leave it just a teeny bit too long and before I know it Storm Ethelred or some such comes along and blows them to an angle from which they never recover; even if I straighten them the next day, they bear the recognisable kink of neglect.

Gardener

Dear Gardener

I do love entertaining but I don't find it really easy, as everyone thinks I do. The key to it all is organisation. I know most of the time I am not very tidy or organised, but when I am planning an event I do make endless lists and notes about how it will all work.

I start with thinking about what would be delicious together and what kind of people are coming. I write down how I want it to look and I also do a cooking plan, with every step written down; a time-plan of how to do it all. So there is no great secret to success here – it's about having an idea or a concept and then planning it – and then doing it! I know it would have been more exciting if I'd said I put on some red sequin shoes and I tap them together three times, turn around twice and – voilà – the room is ready, but as you see, the real explanation is quite dull...

Below is a recipe I call Huntress chicken for no reason apart from the fact that I normally serve it in autumn to a crowd. It's a good recipe for making ahead.

Huntress chicken

SERVES 6

6 chicken breasts
350g (12oz) button mushrooms or chopped regular mushrooms
2 red onions, chopped
4 tbsp vegetable oil
50g (1½ oz) butter
200g (7oz) bacon lardons
4 tbsp flour
1 tbsp redcurrant jelly
600ml (21fl oz) red wine
300ml (10½ fl oz) beef stock
A bouquet garni (1 bay leaf, 1 sprig of thyme or 1 sprig of rosemary – or two of all of them)
Parsley, to garnish

Preheat the oven to 200°C. Put your chicken breasts in an oven tray and roast for about 15 minutes until just cooked. Remove from the oven and turn it down to 160°C.

In a large cast-iron casserole, sauté your mushrooms and onions in the vegetable oil and half the butter. Once they have softened, remove to a dish. Add your bacon lardons to the casserole and fry until cooked.

In another pan, put in the other bit of butter over a low heat and mix in the flour. Cook for one minute and then pour in the wine, stock and redcurrant jelly, basically making a gravy. Add your bouquet garni or choice of herb and bring to the boil, then simmer for 20 minutes over a low heat.

Add your mushrooms and onion to the lardons in the casserole, along with the chicken. Put the lid on and cook in the oven for 30 minutes (or for the same amount of time on the hob over a medium to low heat). If you want your gravy a bit thicker, put some cornflour into a mug, mix in some of your sauce to make a paste, then stir this into the casserole.

Serve with dauphinoise or baked potatoes, green beans or roasted kale.

I was going to give you a recipe for a stuffed shoulder of lamb but then I realised I had only made this about twice myself, as it involves sewing up the shoulder with string. So instead I would recommend the following, which is such good way to cook lamb and very easy to carve up. You will want to ask your butcher to bone the joint for you.

Butterfly leg of lamb

SERVES 6

1.5kg (3lb 5oz) boned shoulder or leg of lamb
2 glugs of olive oil
Juice of one lemon
4 garlic cloves, slivered
A sprig or two of rosemary
2 tbsp redcurrant jelly
200ml (7fl oz) red wine

Marinate the lamb in the olive oil, lemon, garlic and rosemary for as long as you can.

Preheat the oven to 220°C. Put the lamb in a roasting pan, cook in the oven for 20 minutes then remove, spread the redcurrant jelly over the meat and pour the wine into the bottom of the pan. Turn the oven down to 180°C and return the lamb for about another hour, after which it should have had a total cooking time of 20 minutes per 450g plus an extra 20 minutes. Remove from the oven and leave to rest for 10–15 minutes before serving.

In the summer, use the BBQ and serve it with big salads. It takes a little less time in the BBQ so start checking it after just an hour or so. Use the red wine in the marinade here not in the BBQ.

I also love boned chicken, which I marinate as with the lamb then serve with a salsa verde (gherkins, garlic, herbs of any kind, oil and vinegar all whizzed up in a mini processor). For a 1.8kg (4lb) chicken the cooking time is 1–1½ hours at 180°C (nearer the hour if you are doing it on the BBQ). You can also stuff your boned chicken, which I love doing with ricotta, sundried tomatoes, olives and fresh basil. This is really good, and great for a crowd.

Boned chicken with ricotta and sundried tomatoes

SERVES 6

50g (1½ oz) melted butter
1.6kg (3lb 6oz) whole boned chicken

For the stuffing

170g (6oz) ricotta cheese
50g (1½ oz) sundried tomatoes
30g (1oz) olives, sliced
2 tbsp basil, roughly chopped
1 tbsp thyme leaves
50g (1½ oz) white breadcrumbs
1 egg
Salt and pepper

Preheat the oven to 200°C. Melt your butter and press a J-cloth into it until it all the butter has been absorbed. Lay the cloth on a flat surface and put the boned chicken flat on top of it, crossways, cavity-side up. Mix together the stuffing ingredients and put in a long sausage-shape along the centre of your chicken. Roll up the chicken in the cloth and tie at each end like a Christmas cracker. Cook in the oven for about 1 hour 15 minutes, then unwrap and serve. This is also delicious cold, so it's brilliant for a buffet-style lunch.

All these meats are delicious served with small roast potatoes and a red ratatouille. I learned this ratatouille recipe when I was at Leiths Cookery School and have used it ever since. It is such a relief not to have the usual soggy courgettes in it and is SUCH a handy side vegetable to serve as it adds a bit of wetness – in a good way – to a plate.

I reiterate: no soggy courgettes!

Red ratatouille

SERVES 6

2 red onions, sliced
1 garlic clove, sliced
2 aubergines, cut into rounds and then halved
2 red peppers, cut into squares
400g tin chopped tomatoes
½ tsp ground coriander
½ tsp cinnamon (if you fancy – can taste weird to some!)
½ tsp caster sugar
Salt and pepper
Fresh basil (purple if you can get it)

Fry the onions until soft. Add the garlic and cook for a further minute before adding the aubergines, peppers, tomatoes, coriander, cinnamon (if using), sugar and the salt and pepper. Simmer for 20–30 minutes so the veg still has a bite to it. Put in a dish and tear fresh basil all over it before serving. Make sure you season well with salt and pepper. You will be surprised how many people like this!

A more pricy option for entertaining is a filet of beef. To keep it simple you can serve it with some crispy potatoes and green beans with a beef jus – so the main event is expensive but the side dishes cheap, easy and effortless. You can even accompany it with your own home-made horseradish sauce, which makes it look like you have made a superlative effort but is just crème fraîche, a dash of vinegar, freshly grated horseradish, half a teaspoon of English mustard and salt and pepper. Alternatively, for a summer buffet serve it with watercress around the edge of the serving dish and your favourite salads.

Filet of beef

SERVES 10

2kg (4½ lb) beef filet

Preheat the oven to 180°C. Sear the filet in a pan on all sides then put it in the oven for 25 minutes. Take it out, wrap in tinfoil and leave to rest for 30 minutes. If it's still too rare just put it back in the oven for 5–10 minutes.

Lastly, this is so simple, but if you have teenagers and children coming for lunch, homemade burgers are a hit every time and are extremely delicious.

Home-made burgers

SERVES 6

1kg (2lb 2oz) good quality steak mince
2 onions, finely chopped
Salt and pepper
A dash of Worcestershire sauce (optional)

Fry the onions until soft, then add your very good mince, salt and pepper, and a dash of Worcestershire sauce if you fancy. A friend gave me a burger-maker (a white, plastic, round mould), which makes them look very professional as they are all the same size! A complete winner with the young carnivore set.

Serve in a gorgeous bun, perhaps with a slice of cheese melted on the top of the burger. Obviously ketchup, mustard and mayo are required.

Cook

14

Tea and topiary

Dear Gardener,

I am writing to you today to ask you your thoughts on topiary.

You have probably seen that the English Heritage garden at our local train station has a wonderful topiary display of a teapot, a cup and a jug. I'm normally not one for this kind of thing, but every time I go to catch a train I find myself looking at the topiary longingly and secretly wishing I had something similar in my garden. Topiary is clever while at the same time faintly magical and definitely slightly ridiculous. Have you done any topiary in any of the gardens that you have designed? Do you think it is for a bigger-scale garden or can folk with an ordinary garden get away with the odd cockerel?

Tea has always been a favourite luxury of mine. If I'm reading a book which is describing a particular teatime (probably Winnie-the-Pooh going to see Rabbit, or Mr Tumnus's house in Narnia), I find myself fantasising about crumpets dripping in butter, scones with dollops of cream and vibrant strawberry jam, and cake so light it melts in the mouth. The fire is lit and I have a large cup of tea – an English type of 'hygge'; a warm comforting feeling left over from childhood of arriving in a warm, cosy house

TEAPOT TOPIARY

OPEN

STATION CAFE

after a damp autumn walk and then tucking into a delicious afternoon tea. One must not worry about calories at teatime – it would be futile. As a very skinny friend of mine once said, 'You just can't work off a large slice of cake – so don't even try and bother.' Tea can also be a very upmarket affair – a city outing in an elegant hotel with silk curtains, Earl Grey and finger-sandwiches of all sorts. I was at a funeral recently and they went big on finger-sandwiches. I've never seen so many women pounce on those plates. Their eyes lit up as they saw the array of cucumber and ham sandwiches. Forbidden but not forgotten, a sandwich holds a place in most people's hearts.

So what is your favourite thing to eat at four o'clock? Also, do you think my yew hedge would be suitable for a bit of topiary, or perhaps the tree on the left as you go into my garden? I think it's a yew but I couldn't be sure.

Here's to jam tarts and all things nice.

You will not be surprised to hear that I use just one recipe for all my cakes, and that is a Victoria sponge recipe. At cooking school, I got ten out of ten for my Victoria sponge and I don't think I have ever forgotten that – full marks (it was a first and last time) – so I have stayed pretty faithful to the Victoria sponge. If I'm doing coffee cake I just do the same recipe and add instant coffee (4 teaspoons of instant coffee to 1 tablespoon of warm water) but I do use real espresso for the coffee butter icing. Coffee cake probably is my favourite and I love it with walnuts or pecans dotted through it. But here is the original Vicky sponge, so you can adapt it how you wish. I find most of my friends ask for this with strawberry-and-cream filling – it seems to be what they like!

Victoria sponge

MAKES A 20CM ROUND CAKE

225g (8oz) butter, softened
225g (8oz) caster sugar
4 eggs, beaten
225g (8oz) self-raising flour
1–2 tbsp milk
Raspberry jam or whipped double cream and strawberries, to fill

I think the two most important factors in making a successful cake are greasing your tins and making sure your oven is the right temperature. I think always use two sandwich tins so that you can have a top and a bottom – it's just so much easier.

Pre-heat the oven to 180°C and grease your two sandwich tins with butter – just use your butter wrapper with the butter that's left on it, and a bit more if you need it, though I'm quite liberal with the butter at this stage and probably use about 20g of butter for greasing.

Using an electric mixer, cream together the butter and sugar until pale and fluffy, then slowly add the beaten eggs. If the mixture curdles add a tablespoon of flour to the mix. Then add the flour, and a tablespoon of milk if you think it's too thick – you want the mixture to be dropping consistency.

Quickly put equal amounts of the mixture in the tins and put in the oven for 20–30 minutes. The cakes should spring back to the touch when ready. Let them cool in their tins. When completely cool, sandwich them together with raspberry jam – or, as I often do, use whipped double cream and strawberries.

I should point out that I often just bung all the ingredients in a food

processor and do an 'all-in-one' and it always works, though it's maybe not quite as light and fluffy.

To make a groovier-looking cake, stick all sorts of garden flowers into the top of the finished cake – in spring I use camellias and rosemary, and even tulips; in summer I use rosemary with roses and daisies. It makes it look a bit mad but really pretty and original – give it a go!

Cook

Dear Cook,

I'm actually salivating... I think that, in any circumstances, afternoon tea is a way better option than supper. Imagine if, rather than a romantic dinner, you went out for a romantic tea? Or consider the invitation 'Why don't we go back to mine for tea?' A much less alarming option. I'd go for scones and hot cross buns; the latter have to be cold, not toasted, with at least 3mm of butter.

Topiary is a work of patience – in some cases a life's work, so I'm not sure that the cultivation of it is for you and me. But plant nurseries sell fields and fields of fabulous shapes for your delectation – a whole new shopping opportunity. I'd avoid the chess pieces unless you want your garden to look like a Peter Greenaway film – mind you, I quite like the slightly bonkers feel of being surrounded by weirdly shaped trees all taller than your average human. But I'm not generally a fan of novelty shapes – I'd go off them. I do get annoyed when I can't quite identify a topiary shape: I was once in a garden in Gloucestershire where the owner asked, 'Have you seen our elephant?' I nervously cast my eye around, wondering whether they meant a real-life animal of the Indian or African variety. Once I had established that this was probably highly unlikely in Stow-on-the-Wold, I had to quickly and desperately look around among all the amorphous shrubs and blobs in their garden, hoping that my eye would come to rest on the one that was so dear to their heart. I think I spotted a passing seagull and pulled that old trick so beloved of Georgie Pillson ('Oh look! A cow...').

Yew (taxus) is tricky but box (buxus) is also risky, due to pesky caterpillars. If the budget allows, I'd go for yew anytime. That last sentence is safer written than spoken.

Gardener

15

Christmas and embarrassing centrepieces

Dear Gardener,

We all go a bit bonkers at Christmas, don't we? Once-calm, peaceful interiors become manic, overcrowded spaces dripping with tinsel, fairy lights and reindeers made of sticks. Once I even bought a felt moose-head that you hang on the wall, with a bell round its neck. Really? You will be glad to know it has found its way to the garage for ever.

I don't know if it's like this because we've all become so Americanised in the last decade. You know what I mean: baby showers, prom dresses – and Halloween has almost acquired cult status now. The trouble is, if you don't join in you are deemed a bah-humbug type of character who is permanently bad-tempered and mean (American-mean and British-mean).

I was staying with a friend of mine before Christmas. Her house is beautifully decorated – the epitome of chic, with nothing too matchy-matchy. However, for her grande soirée I found her in her very cool kitchen making what can only be described as 'embarrassing centrepieces': tangerines in vases with fairy lights and holly. They could have been described as kitsch, but really

they were just embarrassing. Did I feel like that because centrepieces basically don't have a function? I went to a big party last year and the host had decorated her enormous candlesticks with ivy, which looked stunning – maybe because the candle had the function of lighting up the table. I think candles and flowers are brilliant, but that's where it should stop. Do you have a particular plant or flower that lends itself well to giving the table that wow factor?

You mentioned you made a Christmas pudding last week. I was seriously impressed – I don't think I've attempted that in years. As it's the end of the year, could I ask you for that recipe?

Cook

Dear Cook,

Oh, that Christmas pudding! Religiously(!), I make it every year – the recipe was courtesy of Xanthe Clay in the *Telegraph*, and it's brilliant – and if I can make it, anybody can make it. I throw a few little trinkets in for tradition's sake – threepenny bits and old shillings, and one-pound coins if I'm feeling generous. I've lost count of the number of them I've lost over the years. I tell myself they've probably been thrown away with the wishbones and crappy cracker toys and all the rest of the Christmas table detritus, but I can't help thinking that a couple of them still might be residing in an aged aunt's lower gut.

Betty's traditional Christmas pudding

SERVES 6–8

225g (8oz) raisins
50g (2oz) currants
50g (2oz) glacé cherries
85g (3oz) sultanas
15g (½oz) flaked almonds
100ml (4fl oz) brandy
Zest of 1 orange and juice of half
Zest of 1 lemon and juice of half
50g (2oz) vegetable suet
30g (1oz) wholemeal breadcrumbs
50g (2oz) plain white flour
85g (3oz) light brown sugar
½ tsp mixed spice
¼ tsp ground nutmeg
¼ tsp ground cinnamon
A pinch of ground cloves
2 medium eggs, beaten
½ tsp salt

The day before you make your pudding, place all the dried fruits, the nuts and the fruit zest in a bowl and pour the brandy and fruit juices over them. Toss together lightly, cover with cling film and leave to soak overnight.

The following day, place all the ingredients, including the soaked fruit, in a large mixing bowl and lightly mix together – do this by hand to avoid breaking up the fruit.

Place a small disc of baking parchment in the base of a 1½-pint pudding basin. Fill the basin with the pudding mixture and smooth the top down evenly. The mixture should come up to about half an inch from the top of the basin.

Place another, larger, disc of silicone paper on top of the mixture, then cover the top of the basin with tinfoil and seal tightly.

Put the filled pudding basin in a saucepan, with a long, triple-folded strip of tinfoil under it that comes up both sides – this is to help you lift the boiling-hot basin out of the saucepan once it has steamed. Pour boiling water into the saucepan so that it comes halfway up the pudding basin.

Place a lid on the saucepan and bring it back to the boil, then lower the heat and keep the water at a steady simmer, so the pudding steams, for five hours. Check the water level on a regular basis and top up as necessary with boiling water.

When the time is up, remove the pudding from the pan and allow it to cool completely before wrapping it, still in its basin, in a piece of greaseproof, plus a layer of tinfoil. Store in a cool, dark place and leave for at least a month to mature – six weeks is even better.

On Christmas Day, steam the pudding for a further two hours in a pan with boiling water, as before. Turn out then decorate with a sprig of holly. Warm some brandy in a ladle, tipping it so it flames. Pour over the pudding and rush it to table, remembering to ask someone to turn out the lights before you enter the room.

I don't actually know how anyone finds room for any kind of centrepiece on the Christmas table, embarrassing or otherwise. By the time the plates, the serving dishes and the glasses are out, a mountain of tangerines is, frankly, just going to get in the way. You could, I suppose, go and grab an amaryllis or three from your local plant nursery and place them among the clutter in a jaunty, festive way. You could even be rather postmodern and use poinsettia. When it comes down to it, though, I believe bottles of wine make the best centrepiece, and they're mobile, too, sparking joy wherever they move.

Happy New Year!!!

Gardener

Acknowledgements

An enormous thank you to my parents and my children George and Cecilia for their endless patience and support – you're all brilliant.

Jo

Thank you to all my family and friends. Ardent supporters in particular, Jamie, Kit and Daisy, Diane Paterson, James and Anastasia Baker, Humphrey, Julia M, Cravens, Woods, Meddings, Charlie and Annie Redmayne & everyone who bought lunch with the authors... just all so generous and supportive.

Mary Jane

Index

Supporters

Unbound is the world's first crowdfunding publisher, established in 2011.

We believe that wonderful things can happen when you clear a path for people who share a passion. That's why we've built a platform that brings together readers and authors to crowdfund books they believe in – and give fresh ideas that don't fit the traditional mould the chance they deserve.

This book is in your hands because readers made it possible. Everyone who pledged their support is listed below. Join them by visiting unbound.com and supporting a book today.

Sarah Adams
Linda Adeson
Henrietta Afolami
Jo Ainsley
Amanda Allfrey
Judith Anderson
Charlotte Ansell
Natalie Ashbee
Tamsin Ashworth

Alice Atkinson
Vasa Babic
James Baker
Marko and Janet Balabanovic
Derren Ball
Nina Baxter
Pam Beaugie
The Bell in Ticehurst
Sophia Bennett

Belinda Benton

Claire Birrell

Anna Blaxland

Janice Bridger

Fiona Bruce-Smythe

Selina Bunting

The Byrnes

Anna Canetty-Clarke

Tara Carlisle

William Casement

Debbi Chai

Claire Champon

Gavin Chapman

Annelli Cleverly

Harriet Cleverly

Katie Clifton

Ali Cobb

Maria Cobbe

Jess Cook

David Cooke

Ali Costain

Paddy Coulman

Clare Cowburn Baker

Charlie Craven

Clare Craven

Charlie Crossley Cooke

Celia Crowther

Charlotte Cunningham

Sarah Davies

Jenny de Montfort

Janie Dear

Philippe Demeur

Sarah Densham

Chris Devaney

Mark Diacono

Michael Donovan

Janey Downshire

Katy Driver

David Duffy

Kate Durr

Tomas Eriksson

Marie-Claire Erith

Tim Evans

Virginia Fassnidge

Sally Fincher

Shan Foster

Fenella Fox-Pitt

Joanna Fraser

Tavia Gethin

Olivia Gianelli

Caroline Gibbons

Nick Gibbons

Tamsin Gill

Richard Glynne

Sonia Goodman

Flora Gordon Clark

Meg Gordon Sussman

Sarah Gore

Georgia Greer

Ann Griese

Sarah Gustafson

Alex Hammersley

Claire Hankinson

Lucy Harby

Diana Hardman

Peter Harrison

Alex Hearn

Pam Henderson

Claire Heron

Harriet Hills

Barry Holloway

Polly Holman-Baird

Pippa Horlick

Caroline Hornsby

Jason and Amanda Howard

Claire Hughes

Katharine Hunter

Caroline Hunter Blair

Rachel Hurrell

Patricia Irvine

Nicola Johnson

Alan Johnston

Cathy Jones

John Keeling

Paul Keeling

Tania Keeling

Lottie Keith

Dan Kieran

Jo and Nigel Killick

Daisy L-Paterson

Emily Lampson

Louisa Leader

Catherine Leefe

Lia Leendertz

Phillipa Lepley

Jane Leung

Alison Levey

Kit Lillingston-Paterson

Fiona Lock

Cicely Lowe

Dominic Lowe

Judith Lowe

Mark Lowe

Susan Lowe

Candida Machin

Jonathan Macintosh

Nadine Majaro

Angela Mannis

Lucy McCahon

James McConnel

Sam Mcknight

Heidi Mcneilly

Henrietta Meddings

Cem Meredith

Alice Millar

Louise Minchin

John Mitchinson

Sarah Montague-Wilson

Hazel Moore

Sophie Moreland

Caroline Morris

Non Morris

Julia Mortimer

Fiona Mortimore

Cressida Murray
Carlo Navato
Victoria Neave
Carolyn Nisbet
Humphrey Nokes
Rosie Nottage
Veronica Olszowska
Jennifer Ouvaroff
Sally Painter
Louisa Paravicini
Lev Parikian
Nicky Parkinson
Bettina Pasztor
Diane Paterson
Jamie Paterson
Elizabeth Payne
Poppy Peacock
Robert Peacock
Hugo Perks
Joanna Petty
Maria Pickard
Jacqui Pickles
Kenny Pieper
Yvette Pitchforth
Sophie Plowden
Justin Pollard
Philippa Pollock
Sarah Pope
Helen Pritchard
Dodie Pryke
Sarah Pullen

Joana Redding
Annabel Redmayne
Christine Redmayne
Nicky Reynolds
Ness Ringer
Sally Roberts
Vanessa Roberts
Caroline Robinson
Sarah Robinson
Sarah Robson
Vivienne Rogerson
Joanna Ross
Natacha Russell Woods
Clare Rutherford
Seed
Renato Sementini
Eliza Shaw
Jan Sienesi
Bev Small
Clive Smith
Jade 'Flamingo' Smith
Liz Spicer-Short
Lianne Streek
Emma and Richard Street
Karen Styr
Michael Sweet
Susan Swinburn
Rupert Sydenham
Louisa Symington
Sophie Taylor-Young
Melissa Thistlethwayte

Helen Thompson

Jo Thompson

Vivien Thompson

Debs Tilney

Kirsty Todd

Melanie Todd

Catherine Trotman

Juliet Turner

Anna Vereker

Camilla von Greyerz

Kitty Wakefield

Claire Walford

Jill Ward

Sebastian Warrack

Philippa Williams

Amanda Williams-Thomas

Judith Wilson

Lizzie Wingfield

Sheila Wood

Susan Woods

Jacqueline Woolf

Nicole Woolhouse

Michaela Wright

Nona Wright

Alexis Wylie